HOW [illegible]
55 YEARS *of* MARRIAGE
with an Adulterous Husband

How I Survived 55 Years of Marriage with an Adulterous Husband

written by PEARL J. COLE, Ph.D

How I Survived 55 Years of Marriage *with an Adulterous Husband*

ISBN-13: 978-0-692-97311-0

Written by Pearl J. Cole, Ph.D.

Published by Pearl J. Cole Ministries, Inc.
P.O Box 26757
Jacksonville, FL 32226
Website: www.pearljcoleministries.com

Cover Design, CrunchTime Graphics

Editing, SDR Professional Writing Services

Ordering Information: For details, contact the publisher at the above mailing or website address.

Scripture quotations marked KJV are credited to the King James Version, Public Domain

Printed in the USA: A&A Printing

HOW I SURVIVED 55 YEARS OF MARRIAGE *with an ADULTEROUS HUSBAND* is dedicated to my precious mother and married couples around the world.

TABLE OF CONTENTS

DEDICATION

To my precious and beautiful mother, Christine Swain—you were a mother in Zion and a good earthly mother whom I sheltered from many of my trials in my marriage. I did not want to inflict my hurts and burdens upon you knowing it would have saddened you. In my preaching, teaching, and revealing of certain trials I had gone through, you would ask, *When was that*? or *When did that happen*? You were my mentor and example of a good woman with good morals. You not only had a loving and caring heart, but also a giving spirit.

I honor God and salute you for being the holy woman and mother you were. Although you have gone on to be with the Lord, your memories will last forever in my heart where you will never die. I extend the love back to you where you extended the same to me. You are what every pastor would want in a member. I had the opportunity to watch over your soul and feed you heaven's manna—the gospel truth—for a season in your lifetime. You were a disciple who was very orderly, submissive, and faithful.

My mother would be proud of me writing my story for His glory. She has always been proud of me—her 10-pound baby girl—and my being her pastor. To my mother, Christine Swain.

Married couples, for such a time as this, God has allowed me to write my story for His glory. This book, How *I Survived 55 Years of Marriage with an Adulterous Husband*, is dedicated to married couples who feel they do not love each other any longer and have been sold the lie of divorce by the enemy of their souls—the old devil. Yet, deep within, they do and most times after divorced, realize they still want to be with each other only to find out it was a trick of the devil.

This book will help married couples to understand and exemplify God's unconditional love for their mates. It also paints a picture of a true account of how I survived 55 years of marriage to an unfaithful man whom I loved unconditionally with an everlasting love as Jesus forever loves us.

Women, this book will show you how to be the helpmeet that your husband needs. You will learn how to not stop loving him in spite of his need for more women to be attracted to him. My story is to be a testimony to married couples who are struggling in their marriage. I voice today that you can make it if you try with the decision *I can't stop loving you.*

God says let the redeemed say so. We overcame, so we say so. We made a decision that we can't stop loving each other in spite of and love never fails.

To married couples who know you love each other, but the waves of sinful affairs have engulfed your territory of faithfulness and you don't know how to fight and push those waves back from your married life, I dedicate this book to you.

The Holy Spirit, through his Word, taught me how to survive a marriage with many rough waves in it, but yet be reconciled to my mate and has given me the Ministry of Reconciliation. Thus, I am compelled to tell my story for His glory. I realized if I wanted to show up at the graduation, I had to pass my test.

Love Always,
Pearl J. Cole, Ph.D

FOREWORD

While there are many manuscripts written on the topic of marriage, Mother Pearl Cole's book, *How I Survived 55 Years of Marriage with an Adulterous Husband*, demonstrates a woman's strength in the midst of storms and ultimate victory over her enemies. Her personal accounts of the highest institution ordained by God commands attention and respect. Filled with infidelity, pain, and anguish, Mother Pearl Cole's 55-year journey in marriage has been steered by God. Through it all, she remained steadfast, unmovable, and unshakable. Her personal anecdotes and survival strategies provide a blueprint for all dealing with the realities of infidelity. Such strategies are applicable to multifaceted dilemmas in marriage.

Hebrews 13:4 states marriage is honourable in all, and the bed undefiled: but whoremongers and adulterers God will judge. In accordance with scripture, the marriage bed is righteous and unpolluted when shared by a married couple; adulterers are not allowed or welcomed. There are consequences when the marriage vows are broken and adulterers choose to defy the bed that God himself sanctified. The stakes are higher when the participating adulterer is a public worker. Yes, Mother Pearl was cheated on by her husband who is also a public worker. This sweet and praying woman proudly took her marriage vows in the sight of God and a cloud of witnesses with every intention on being a praiseworthy, Proverbs 31 woman. Like her, her husband took a vow to love, protect, honor, and be faithful to her; yet, he often found himself in the hotbed of adultery with different women. One can only imagine the pain and anguish and embarrassment Mother Pearl endured. Rest assure, God was always there and the consequences were stiff.

Although painful in nature, Mother Pearl opens the most personal book of her life to both instruct and encourage others that through God, all things are possible. Mother Pearl's transparent life lessons morph into practical steps for surviving one of the most horrific occurrences one can face in life: infidelity. The book encourages all married couples to think and act counterintuitively to strengthen, repair, and revive their marriages and themselves. The moral of the story is that no matter how terrible the act or who is involved, we must pray continually, trust in God always, and have faith in His master plan.

As a Prophet, I highly recommend Mother Pearl J. Cole's *How I Survived 55 Years of Marriage with an Adulterous Husband.* If there were ever a time when Christian couples need to be aware of the attacks against marriage and the family and how to deal with them, that time is now. I applaud Mother Pearl for her transparency and courage in sharing her personal story that will surely result in strengthening Christian marriages at all levels and serve as a warning to those who attempt to infiltrate them in any way.

Prophet Brian Carn

INTRODUCTION
ABUSE WITH A GLORIOUS END

Fifty years ago, I heard the Lord calling me out of darkness into holiness up on the King's highway. I came running out of the world into the house of God surrendering my total life to Christ not desiring to hold any of myself back. With everything within me, I gave God me. I had a strong desire to live right. I believed being a Christian was to be different, Christlike, and that gave me an unction to do what He says for us to do.

I heard God speaking in Ephesians 5:27 through a 14-year-old young man who was preaching that Christ will present to himself a glorious church not having spot or wrinkle or any such thing, but it should be holy and without blemish. I wanted to be a part of that glorious church and therefore I took heed to my ways and became a part of his sanctified, cleansed with the washing of water by the word church. My marriage was in trouble at that time, but the devil came against my marriage in greater ways. Yet, I never charged God foolishly. I never believed God was the author of my troubled marriage. I believe He was the sustainer and finisher of my faith. So, I began to practice the principles of the gospel, which are grace and truth. According to the scripture, grace and truth came by Jesus Christ. Thy word is truth. I stood on the written Word. I began to suffer many more trials in my marriage, and at that time, my husband was not a believer. He was not born again of the Spirit of God and he was being untrue to our marriage committing adultery. For many years, I've valued my dedication to God where I did not want to displease God nor my husband; therefore, I dealt with my husband through God's grace and truth.

Grace is the love of God shown to the unlovely; the peace of God given to the restless. Grace is God doing good for us that we do not deserve. You can't earn God's grace. I ministered the word of God by God's grace and my marriage, and many others', were saved and blessed. I kept my destiny in view by fulfilling my purpose. I realized marriage was not a stop in the bedroom only, but a stop at the heart with the decision to love your spouse as the Bible says to do.

I learned how to love an unlovable spouse and be rewarded on this side of glory. Even through the troublesome marriage, there was much reconciliation all because the spirit of humility was manifested all throughout the marriage from the one who had the greater One inside of her heart—me. Through my chaste conversation, which was my conduct, my husband slowly began to change.

I asked my husband, "What happened to make you change?" He replied, "You; it was how you put up with my foolishness. I would do things to make you angry, but you would not stay angry long and I saw what a good wife I had to put up with that." I was a great inspiration to him the way I lived the life of Christ and most of all, God saved him.

This is why I am inspired to write my life story on marriage and how I survived with 55 years invested. It was by the grace of God I am what I am. Others survived their marriage and God favored them and blessed them abundantly through my story. I tell my story for His glory!

I kept the love chapter in my heart; 1 Corinthians 13:8 says love never fails; you as an individual fail. I knew, according to Psalm 126:5-6, that distress will not last always and forever. I kept in remembrance 'there is work to do' whether I am emotionally up for it or not. Tears and all will bring a harvest of blessings. Sow in tears, you'll reap in joy! Your tears will turn to joy—look for it!

I had many nights of wet pillow tears; now, I have many nights of dry pillow rest. I am reaping my greatest harvest. As I sit and write this book from home, I am constantly being served by my husband. He is cooking and serving me breakfast and has my coffee brewed every morning. Before leaving for work, my cup and spoon are left in front of the sugar dish, so when I do arise to come in the kitchen, it is all there for me. When he is off, it is brought to me in my bed or to the kitchen table. As I served him at home wherever he sat when he was so unlovable, he does the same for me. If it is a weekday or weekend he has off from work, I am served lunch and dinner.

Whenever he comes in for a morning break, if I desire breakfast by his hands, he cooks it for me and serves it to me. Yes, he has spoiled me, but you must remember, I well know that a wife is to take care of her husband and I have served my time in doing so. My husband's life, in return, is making me happy to get everything done for me around the house. His words are, "Whatever I hear you saying that needs to be done, I feel good in doing it for you." It is his choice. You must keep in mind that this is the heart of a man who was unfaithful to his wife for so many years and she was aware of it. He does everything for me now; it is his way of showing me his gratitude.

He is so thankful to God for forgiving him for all of his wrongdoings and that he had a wife who prayed God's blessings on him and forgave him for all he had done to her. 2 Corinthians 5:17-18 says "therefore if any man be in Christ, he is a new creature; old things are passed away; behold, all things are become new. And all things are of God who hath reconciled us to himself by Jesus Christ, and hath given to us the ministry of reconciliation."

RECONCILIATION: THE RESTORATION OF FRIENDLY RELATIONS

I made it my priority to reconcile. I made sure I ministered grace and love to my husband. When there were different opinions, marital discord, and our hearts were being pulled apart, I had an urgency to always forgive especially if asked.

> Then came Peter to him, and said, Lord, how oft shall my brother sin against me, and I forgive him? till seven times? Jesus saith unto him, I say not unto thee, Until seven times: but, Until seventy times seven.
>
> – Matthew 18:21-22

Seventy times seven equates to 490 times or indefinitely. We must always forgive; the scripture does not include an excuse for unforgiveness.

> Hatred stirreth up strifes: but love covereth all sins.
>
> –Proverbs 10:12

Love enables us to forgive all sins over and over again. The term forgive is a word that was made up of the words force and giving. Together, they describe forgiveness as the process whereby the offended party gives up the rights to enforce justice. These were some of my reasons for feeling inspired to write my marital life story. It indeed helped me and others to succeed and forgive. Therefore, I feel led to carry it to the nations. God brought me out. The work He started in me, He finished it because I allowed him to do so.

I am here to say I could not cut the umbilical cord because it is cut at birth. For my husband, there had not been a spiritual birth yet; therefore, in spite of circumstances, I felt obligated to stay connected to him; that he be nurtured with my blood supply from the word of God; that he receive food and oxygen and life be ministered unto him from the umbilical cord. I had a commitment to carry him until he could breathe and live on his own. I was my Brother's Keeper to my husband.

I took care of him spiritually looking out for his soul salvation. I prayed and prayed for my husband until a transformation took place and it was not overnight nor yesterday, but it took yesteryears. To God be the glory!

THE DEVIL AND I HAD A TUSSLE. I WON.

I felt pressed to write my story for the Lord enabled me to love the unlovable. Others heard and knew of my story and marveled over it; then, encouraged me to write and tell it—especially my niece Carol. Down through the years, she was with me as I journeyed on to win this battle. My mission and assignment then and now is to encourage women not to throw away their marriage over an incident or incidents if any way possible. You can exchange the pot for the kettle and the pot doesn't cook always, but the kettle does nothing, but boil water.

FORGIVE

Forgiveness is not easy nor are we willing to forgive most times. It is difficult being the recipient of the hurt and pain and then be asked to forgive. In some situations, people never forgive, but this is not the word of the Lord. It was difficult for me too because my husband was not always the loveable man God has transformed him into today. Yet, the word of God kept me forgiving with scriptures from the Bible—Romans, Job, and Hebrews. There are charges we will not be able to execute in our flesh; we need the power of God and His word to equip us to do all things including forgiving our trespassers.

Romans 5:8-10 teaches me to love as Christ for he loved us in spite of us and our sins and died while we were still in the midst of it, so that we can be reconciled unto him.

> But God commendeth his love toward us, in that, while we were yet sinners, Christ died for us. Much more then, being now justified by his blood, we shall be saved from wrath through him. For if, when we were enemies, we were reconciled to God by the death of his Son, much more, being reconciled, we shall be saved by his life.
>
> –Romans 5:8-10

Job 14:1 helped me to release my spirit to know that the devil had touched my marriage and brought trouble to it.

"Man that is born of a woman is of few days and full of trouble." That is what Job said. I, in return, said since the devil brought trouble into my marriage, I am determined to see God heal my troubled marriage and He did. I stood on the written word to see it come alive in my life. Destiny is fulfilling your purpose. I could not minister life and forgiveness to the world and not to my husband.

I had to realize that, somehow, I got to make this journey by dying to my flesh and knowing that my marriage is a heart walk and that light needed to show up. No matter how I was mistreated and misused, I was required to do the right thing. Sin for a season is just not worth the debt that has to be paid. Love saved me—God's love. I rendered love back to my husband. I stayed at the altar; at the altar is change. You come to the altar to change from two to one in marriage.

Some of you have not been in the storm yet, but some of you get married and end up in the storm. Let me encourage you—wear the storm. You will be blessed behind the storm. I can report from a troublesome marriage that was filled with infidelity, my husband desired to stay married and by the grace of God, I suffered it to be so. Now, I am reaping great benefits for I know according to Hebrews 10:37 that "For yet a little while and he that shall come will come, and will not tarry."

I counsel not myself. I allowed the word to counsel me. I kept my eyes on my purpose and destiny, not my pain. Yes, you may say I was a fool, but I was a fool for Christ. I learned how to submit to an unsaved husband. I paid my tithes and gave my offerings and God was obligated to me. He rebuked the devourer for my sake and honored me and my marriage. My prayer is that God continues to bless him and give him long life.

Through what I suffered, I experienced God in a greater way. Through those dark and weary days, I went to school. What enabled me is that I kept focused and placed God first. I believe that is why the enemy fought me so hard; he knew God was first in my life, so he made my plight worse and worse. You must have a strong dedication to God. Out of all I was going through, God was still moving on my behalf.

As you read this book, allow the word of God to minister to your hearts and marriage. Allow Him to restore what was, so that you can experience true love in the Master and your marriage. Re-dedicate yourselves and marriage to Him; lay it at His feet—at the altar and watch Him take that broken thing and make it beautiful.

God can use all things for His glory. He is the Author and Finisher of my faith. God has paid me well.

CHAPTER ONE
MY MARRIAGE

At the age of 17, I married my husband before the Justice of the Peace not knowing God and neither did my husband. Our marriage was not solid because of other women being in his life. Again, I was 17 and he was 25 when we got married.

It was on a Sunday morning. I was pregnant having only three months before delivery. I wore a new chocolate brown maternity dress with a gold necklace and gold slippers. He had on a pair of trousers and a short sleeve shirt. I had no wedding party; no mother or father in attendance. Only my sister Lucille and my two nieces Sharon and Donna attended and they were my witnesses.

We took our vows not understanding the real meaning of holy matrimony. Some predicted that the marriage would last only for three months. We married on September 2, 1962. Now, it is 2017—look at God! For He is my survival kit and much more.

OUR EARLY MARRIAGE

At that time, I did not know the sincerity and value of the marriage vows. We were young, foolish, blind, and unlearned without marriage counseling and unsaved.

After the ceremony at the Justice of the Peace, my husband dropped me off to my mom's house and he went out to his mom's house; they lived down the street from each other. It was not until later in the evening that we went home to our one-bedroom occupant at a rooming house.

I went into a marriage of infidelity knowing, so there was no true happiness. I did what I felt I needed to do to stop bringing shame to my mom's house. We had one child, our first-born out of wedlock, and in six months of the next year, we were expecting our second child. That following year, our third child was born and that brought on more stress, anxiety, and financial problems. It got to the place where lesser attention was on me, not necessarily because of the babies, but because of his involvement with outside women.

Unfaithfulness was what I breathed day after day and night after night and for months and years. He gave very little time to the children for he was too busy taking care of business with his company of ladies on the outside, so he had little energy left for the children. He had a routine schedule for his everyday lifestyle. First, he left home very early in the mornings to do outside house runs before work. Next, he stopped by certain places before coming home. Third, he came home to take a nap because he worked split shifts. Fourth, he went back to work. Five, he came home at the end of the day and rested up to finally go back out to do house runs outside again.

Our marriage immediately grew worse and cold. I began to feel more unhappy because I felt hurt all the time and betrayed. Yet, he was so jealous and I had such a hard time getting to where I needed to go because of his jealousy. He forbid that I would get rides with male friends or even speak to them. In our early marriage, we only had the one car and there was a period of time with no car and really, he was not anxious about getting me a car. I guess he was afraid that I would run up on him out there in those streets—places he should not have been. He even had some girlfriends right in our neighborhood. Anyway, I had to get a bus or a cab to get to my destinations.

One day, I was trying to get to a doctor's appointment. After waiting for a cab so long, a family member and co-worker saw me standing on the streets and offered to give me a ride. I accepted it, but one of my husband's brothers saw me and reported it to him. My actions caused my husband to be so upset where he made it clear and understandable that I was not to take any rides with a male simply because he had two failed marriages and on my watch, I had to pay for the mistakes of his previous two wives. By the way, I was pregnant with our fourth child.

The early part of our marriage, we went to church sometimes, not all the time. Remember, he was so jealous where I could not go anywhere freely not even to church. He was afraid to trust me, yet he was untrustworthy and I knew it, but I just felt in my spirit to keep my marriage. My life was miserable, but not tormenting. I was not at liberty to go out and have fun. He would not carry me any place for entertainment. I became an old lady at a very young age. All fun things like concerts, dances, restaurants and eating out, partying with friends—none of that we did together. He would go alone and do his thing leaving me home with frustration building up.

My bedtime became very early. Most times, around 8:00 p.m., the house would be shut down only when he would go out on weeknights and some weekends. He had a way about him where he was an early riser because of early hours on the job and he was trying to go to bed early. He had a split shift job for a long time, so he knew how to make early house runs in between outside house runs and late in the evening outside house runs. He had a regular pattern and I was not ignorant of what was going on. I had a grace to keep my marriage—the little I had. Remember, I had not given my life to Christ yet, but there was always a stirring in my heart for the Lord.

CHAPTER TWO

MY UNSAVED DAYS

During my early married and unsaved days, many, many unpleasant things happened in our marriage. I remember my husband went out one night and had to knock on the front door for me to let him in. I opened the door being very angry with him. I met him at the door with a kitchen knife and as he walked in, I dashed at him with the knife and scraped his hand a little. He ran to my mom's house to report me to her and to get some help with his finger, which was bleeding a little. My mom bandaged up his finger and he came back home and went to bed falling asleep leaving me angry and frustrated with him. I had so many nights, days, months, and years with an aching, hurt heart, and a frowned face at such a young age.

Around the age of 19, another thing occurred and now, as I look back, I actually see how dumb it was. Anyway, on this particular day, my husband was off from work. He carried me to my mom's and he left, being gone for a long time. I decided to walk to a place not too far from my mother's house where he would hang out sometimes. This place was a juke place and over it were rooms where people lived. I had seen him up those stairs before, but this particular day, he was on the ground sitting in a chair lying back surrounded by two women. One was leaning over him mashing a bump in his face and there was much laughter and fun going on. Someone spotted me and let him know I was across the street looking on. Well, he raised up his head and called out to me. I did not answer him for I did not want him to see me, so I hid behind a telegram pole. At the moment, that was all I could hide behind. There was nothing else that I could hide behind. That was another hurt and revealing moment. I knew he would be up there so much and mostly upstairs and on the grounds of that juke place with these two women around him or at least one of them keeping him company. These are just a few troublesome things that happened in our early marriage.

Now, you know there was no trust in the marriage even from the beginning. I admonish you not to go into a marriage with no trust. It is too devastating. You can lose your mind over that. If it had not been for the grace of God, I would have lost mine. Yet, I was faithful to my husband.

Yes, I birthed him seven children and had one miscarriage at the age of 30. I had five boys and two girls—my first born at the age of 16. While in the rooming house living upstairs, I'm at the age of 18 almost 19, our oldest child was at home living with my mother. Our second child was with us in the rooming house and we had a third child on the way. We were very young with no real good paying job at the time and things were a little rough. I had no car, so I would sometimes walk from 5th Street to 25th Street with child. After the baby was born, I would walk sometimes with my baby as far as to 8th Street and then get a cab or bus and get off, or out, at 25th Street to my mom's house. Well, while on 5th Street, my third child was born, so I remember days when I would have one of my little girls by the hand and the youngest one in my arms and walk until a bus or cab came along. Many times, I was talked about by the bus passengers and cab drivers, but I held on to my husband, my babies, and my life.

HIS JEALOUSY

My husband did not want me to be friendly with other women either especially where we lived in the rooming house. Finally, we moved from the 5th Street rooming house to a duplex with a living room, one bedroom, and kitchen and bathroom. While there, we had our 4th child. That's when I began to miss my teenage life. There was a young lady who lived next door and I wanted to go with her to a concert, but my husband did not want me to go along with her and he would not carry me. I begged and asked could I go for a whole week. Finally, he let me go with all kinds of rules and orders to follow, but he, on the other hand, would go out by himself. One day on a Saturday, he went out and when he came home, he fell out on the floor pretending to be drunk. I decided I would cuss him for as long as I felt like it simply because I could not beat him, so I decided I would cuss him out until I felt better. My reason was that I was always left home attending to the babies, changing diapers, cooking and cleaning, and washing clothes; therefore, I was very frustrated and he would not help me much at all, so I exploded that day. It was in the summertime and my landlord lived next door. My window was up; I was angry and loud and cussing with a loud voice. I cussed and cussed. Remember, I was not saved yet. Finally, my landlord came to my window and asked me to stop. Naturally, I stopped, but I became angry at her too, so I soon moved.

THE ROOMING HOUSE

At the rooming house on 5th Street, our occupant was upstairs and kitchen downstairs. There were times I would have to leave the two girls, who were my two babies 11 months apart, upstairs alone to warm milk or cook. Most times, I would wait until they fell asleep to go downstairs. One day, coming back upstairs, I heard my youngest baby crying hysterically. I rushed to the bedroom and as I entered, I did not see her, but I could hear her. Yet, I could not pinpoint right away where the sound of her voice was coming from. I guess because it was muzzled and the television was on. Finally, I started searching for her again and I could not find her immediately. Remember now, I'm around 18, done had my third child, frustrated every day over my married life situation and may as well say taking care of two babies, so I guess my head wasn't on just right. I did, however, find my baby on the floor in between the bed and wall near the window with the curtains swaying over her face. By that time, I was hysterical. See, what had happened was the baby rolled off the bed while I was downstairs. I had taken her from the bassinet. Remember, this was back in the 60s. Yes, I was a young mother, but I loved my children and I rescued my baby and loved on my other little girl who was asleep too, but by the time I got through hollering "Where is my baby?," she was awakened also. It was just like having two babies for they were only 11 months apart. My unsaved days were tough. I was living life and had not yet found Christ.

CHAPTER THREE

MY SAVED LIFE

The house we moved into was a pretty nice looking house. It was freshly painted with large rooms and my children had a room. What I did not know until after moving in the house is that it had mice. I was very unhappy in that house, but that's the house where I met Jesus and surrendered my life to him. Before I tell you about my saved life, let me say this: Yes, my husband was whorish, but I do believe he loved his family including me. He took us on vacation every summer; he worked and took care of us well. Yes, there were times his girlfriends would buy Christmas gifts or let him use their account to get toys for the boys, such as bicycles and household items like a television, freezer, and other things, for the family. Still, his personality and character were mean-spirited. I was not an angel, but I was a good girl and he had a lot of good in him as well that God would soon allow to surface.

I was raised in the church from a child and the Lord touched my life mightily as a girl around 12 years old. The Holy Spirit fell upon me at a neighborhood prayer group and all members were old besides me. It consisted of my mother, two sisters, mother-in-law, and father-in-law, but they weren't my in-laws at that time for I was only around 12 years of age.

After that great experience, Satan came in my life for a season. I had no one to teach me the Bible—God's word, so I failed to follow on, but I always had a hunger and thirst for the living God. I felt the call of God on my life in my childhood days. My desire was to be a missionary in Africa, but I remember that I always told God I would give him my life when I reached age 21. So, at the age of 21, I got down on my knees to receive Christ and the old devil got down with me and frightened me. I got up and told God I would do it next year at the age of 22. The grace and mercy of God let me live and saved me at the age of 22.

MY CONVERSION

It was on the first Sunday night of September in 1966 when God visited me in a powerfully strange way. I had been at church that Sunday morning. A woman at the church asked me to go to another church with her that evening for communion. Although my husband did not allow me to go to church twice on Sunday, by the grace of God, I was able to go.

After leaving the communion service with her, there was a late evening service at our church, so I stopped there too. They had a young 14-year-old boy to bring the word, but the devil tried to stop the plan of God by putting a stumbling block in his way. The young boy had no transportation. On Sundays, cabs and buses ran slow and he had a time trying to get a cab to bring him from the Eastside to the Northside where the church was located. We did not think he would make it, but when we were about to give the benediction, he walked in the door.

He was allowed to speak and he preached a message concerning the church that God was going to present to himself; how it will be glorious without spot or wrinkle. My heart was pricked and he went on to include Psalm 40:1-3.

I waited patiently for the LORD; and he inclined unto me, and heard my cry. He brought me up also out of a horrible pit, out of the miry clay, and set my feet upon a rock, and established my goings. And he hath put a new song in my mouth, even praise unto our God: many shall see it, and fear, and shall trust in the LORD.

–Psalm 40:1-3

The power of God came upon me that evening in the service and I tried to shake it off. I stopped by some friends' house and began to joke and play around with them thinking the conviction was going to leave me, but it didn't. When I got home around 8:00 that night, a radio pastor from the city came on the air and God used him to say to me, "sometimes you are on the wrong train; you have to get off one train and get on another.

Sometimes you are on the wrong train; you have to get off one train and get on another.

By that time, the power of the Holy Ghost fell on me and the brightness of His glory lit up all around me. It shine so bright and all I could do was yield myself to His power. Great conviction came over me and I could understand what the Holy Spirit was saying to me. It was like that night, he said, "I have come for you to give yourself completely to me." My heart, mind, soul, and body were yielded saying yes. Tears were running as I was under arrest by the Holy Spirit and I did not fight it; I wanted it. I needed it. I gladly received it. That was the night I gave my life to Jesus Christ. I surrendered all to him. I have never desired to walk away from my Lord. Never! God was so in control and I was such a yielded vessel that it frightened my husband. He ran and got my mother and said to her, "Something is happening to that girl. You need to come and see."

My mother entered my bedroom and I was still engulfed with the Lord's presence. She spoke softly and said, "God has special people and you are one." After that glorious experience, the Holy Spirit instructed me to go to the holiness church where the young man was a member and I did. The next Sunday, which was the second Sunday, also youth Sunday, I showed up and gave my testimony. I told the pastor and congregation how the young preacher up there in the choir stand had blessed my soul and I was coming to join the church. With amazement, the pastor called on the young preacher to bring the message that morning. It was a glorious day and I went to the altar after the message and the Lord poured out His Spirit on me again. Something new and different had come over me, which was new life. My husband sensed it, so he followed me to church that Sunday morning; however, he didn't understand the power of God being all upon me and my falling at the altar under the power of God, so he rushed from his seat to come and see about me to try and pick me up. The missionaries assured him I was all right and that the Lord was dealing with me. When we got home from church service, he made it known that he did not like what took place in church; he did not like me being on the floor and my hair being 'messed up' as he called it.

The next Sunday, he did not come to the church service, but he brought me and the children. I had four children. At the time, 2 girls, 2 boys, and my baby at that time was around 6 months old. We had to stand outside of the church until prayer was over and it so happened that the young 14-year-old preacher was at the door waiting also and he was so happy to see me. Therefore, he turned around to me and gave me what was called a holy greeting with a kiss on the cheeks. My husband had not pulled off yet and he did not like it. He was bothered by that and by the sisters in the church giving me a holy kiss greeting. He claimed one sister kissed me on the lips. Satan, the accuser was there to point out everything to bring an accusation against the saints to make it look like there were some funny ladies in the midst. My mind, instead, was elevated on spiritual things and not on things of the flesh.

My dedication was strong, unmovable to always abound in the work of the Lord. I began to seek the ways of God and the missionaries let me know that I needed the Holy Ghost on my saved life; that He would give me power to live right and within myself. I said a resounding "Yes! Yes!" That is what I needed because my biggest issue was my nasty mouth of cussing. I told the Lord, "Yes, Lord I need the Holy Ghost because I need power over my mouth to stop cussing." I began to avail myself for the church services that were rendered there at the church. There was Bible Study each Tuesday night; Tuesday Morning Prayer Service; Thursday Noonday Prayer Service; and Friday Night Tarry Service, which was a service where the congregation would assemble in praying, singing, testifying, teaching, and healing. We were taught to believe God and wait on His manifestations and that is what I did.

One Friday night, our pastor had a prayer line service and he instructed us that whatever it was that we needed from the Lord to believe Him for it. As he would pray for us, he anointed us with oil as we would go through the prayer line and would teach us to believe the touch of the presence of the Lord; believe God is doing it for you especially when you feel the presence and power of the Lord. He taught us faith more than feeling because you can feel God's presence, but if you don't receive His word in your heart, you still won't receive His blessings. This Friday night, during Prayer and Tarry Service, I went through the prayer line to receive the gift of the Holy Ghost. As the pastor anointed my forehead with oil and told me to believe, I did just that. I believed God for the Holy Ghost. Now, we were taught that the evidence of being baptized or filled with the Holy Ghost was the speaking in other tongues as the Spirit of God give the utterance and I knew that, but as I believed God that night for the Holy Ghost, I felt nothing, but I gave God praise for the Holy Ghost anyway. Now, remember, service on Friday night was Tarry Service where we would go to the altar and pray, surrender, and bless God and wait for manifestation. We would leave the altar believing and trusting God to do what we asked Him to do for the word tarry means to wait. I left service with gladness in my heart knowing that sooner or later, the Holy Ghost was going to fall upon me with the speaking in other tongues as the Spirit gives me the utterance as in Acts 2:4. It did not happen in service that

Friday night nor Saturday nor Sunday, but I kept the faith and praised God for the Holy Ghost. On that 3rd day, which was Monday morning, I got on my knees to pray and bless God because we were taught to pray and praise; to praise God for what you are waiting for, so I did. I began to praise God for the Holy Ghost and suddenly, the Holy Ghost came upon me with my speaking in other tongues, which was heavenly.

I fell in love with Jesus to serve him the rest of my days. I gave up the world to follow Jesus. At the age of 22, I dropped my dress length from up over my knees to mid-length down my legs, took off low cut dresses—now that was my dedication unto the Lord. My hunger for God was where I had to be to prayer service and Bible teachings, I would ask co-workers on the job to change days with me, so I could be off on prayer days in the day time.

I was going through so much in my marriage where I needed God and wanted Him. There were times I just wanted to go on and be with the Lord because of the hurt and mistreatment, but deep down inside, I knew I had a purpose and I needed to fulfill my purpose in life. I began to run for my life and not look back.

My husband did not understand my dedication; he would see men and women at the church on weekdays as I would go to pray and seek the Lord. Sometimes, it would be from 10:00 in the morning to 12:00 in the afternoon; maybe sometimes longer if people were on the altar seeking salvation or to be baptized in the Holy Ghost; you must remember, that was the old-school way, but it was a good way; it worked for those of us who embraced it.

My husband began to question me. "Why do ya'll stay in there so long—all shut-in in there?" Well, what he did not know was that the door was not locked; whosoever wanted to come and pray and seek the Lord was welcomed. It worried his spirit where he said, "I'm coming up there to see what's going on." I replied, "Come and see."

He walked through the door one day on a Tuesday morning around 10:30 or 11:00 and to his surprise, the brethren who were there invited him to the altar. Now, that was not his real reason for coming; his real reason was that he wanted to see why we stayed so long. Well, what he didn't know is that we had praise service, testimony service, Bible teaching, and altar call—just on the altar crying out to God. Those were the ways we were strengthened in God and how we grew in Him. Now, back at the altar with my husband, he said he wanted prayer to be saved, so he was asked to go to the altar. He kneeled at the altar and the men began to pray with him, but they kept him down there too long for he had to go back to work. That didn't wear too well with him because he really came to see what happens in there anyway. He did not come back to that morning prayer.

MEAN-SPIRITED

My husband was mean-spirited. He was so mean until my friends and the children's friends were reluctant to call the house. One of his nieces would hope that he did not answer the phone when she called. Well, we were so used to him and his mean spirit where it was normal to us. If he acted any differently, then we would have been surprised. The children's friends would tell them they were afraid to call the house because their daddy would answer the phone with a mean tone. Even some of my friends would hang up because of the hostility in his voice. Years later, my husband accepted Christ and one of my close saintly friends said to me, "Missionary Cole, God had to do something for your husband because he was so hostile and mean till he would cause me to become mean." It was the way he would answer the phone. He carried deep frowns in his face; they were so deep, he himself tried to hide them by wearing a cap on his head with a bib. He just did not carry a pleasant look, but after he accepted Christ, his countenance changed. Also, he has a different spirit today and people cannot believe he is the man we speak about.

My worship was for real. I found out that prayer is the hand that moves the word and when we hear from God, we have an advantage over the natural man. Those are just some of the ways of how I survived 55 years of marriage with my adulterous husband.

CHAPTER FOUR
MY HUSBAND'S AFFAIRS

After giving my life to Christ—notice how I say that—*I gave my life to Christ*—meaning all of me. I wasn't willing to hold back any of me. I sold out to Christ. I had the cross before me and the world behind me not to turn back. Being 22, I was very unhappy being unsaved and married, so I decided I was going to be saved and happy. I had so many trying times learning about women being in my husband's life such as one giving him a job as a yard man where she worked as a maid; he carried our boys with him to help do the yards and later going by the maid's house after getting off. Those were things our sons experienced. One of his girlfriends worked at a clothing store and purchased him a navy blue suit for his father's funeral. It was a very good looking suit. Later on in our marriage, he brought home some very nice undershorts and I knew immediately that he had not picked them himself because they were too fancy. When I asked him about the shorts, he said he bought them, but the Holy Spirit let me know, he did not.

A few days later, he was at home taking his evening nap as usual and later getting up to make his runs, or his house runs, as I call them. As he was in the bed, the phone rang, but he had retired for the night. When the phone rang, I answered and it was a lady on the line and she told me to tell Cole to give her the money for the undershorts and she hung up. I delivered the message to him. He immediately rose from napping and put on his clothes in a rage and left the house. Upon his arrival back home, I asked, "Why did you have to go off? He just ignored my questions and went back to bed. I knew he did not like her calling his home, so he had to attend to that situation right away. Keeping my praise hot is how I survived all of those hostile acts; I kept thanksgiving on my lips and a dance of victory in my feet and at the same time, God was anointing me a fresh day by day; my inward man was being renewed.

I stayed around the mother of the church; going to different deliverance services, constantly being encouraged by the mothers, saints, missionaries, and ministers. Everybody did not know my story or what I was going through, but those who did were praying mothers and saints of the household of faith.

I remember one night, I was coming home from work and it was around 8:00 in the evening and I had no car of my own. Therefore, I was riding with a co-worker and I had asked her to drop me off at church because we were having church service that night. Just one block from the church, I happened to look down the street and there was my husband putting a lady out who lived about one block around the corner from the church. It was dark and away from the church, but the Lord allowed me to see that. I knew of the lady. She was not a bosom friend nor a friend at all, but he would hang around her house, which was a rooming house, and I knew her name and she was friendly towards me whenever we would meet up. He became a perpetual liar. He lied and said someone asked him to carry her some place, but if that were true, he would not have had to put her off down the street. Well, he said her boyfriend would not have liked it. I did not stop. I went on in church and let the Lord bless me real good. I kept myself in church and in the presence of the Lord because my life was full of disappointments and mistreatment. I used to wonder who I was sometimes. I wondered who was Mrs. Cole because I didn't feel like her neither was I treated like her.

As time pressed on, I realized I needed all the Jesus I could get, so we would have revival services at the church and I would attend; the service would be so good and fulfilling, but my husband had given me a curfew to be home at 10:00 p.m. If I missed curfew, the night latch would be on and I would have to beg him to let me in. There were a few mothers and missionaries who knew my curfew and I lived only about five minutes from the church. If I did not have my car, which was his car, for we only had the one car at the time, I would have to ask a sister in the church to carry me home. Remember, these were the days of yesterday in the 70s, 80s, and 90s where we addressed one another as Sister and Brother and Mother. Listen, the revival service would be so good where I would be willing to pay the cost of being late which would be my key would not work because of the night latch that had been put on the door. Because I had not arrived and my curfew had passed, the door would be locked. If the door was locked, I would beg to be let inside the house.

I would be pulled out of bed after having to beg to get inside the house, so I could go to bed. My words would be, "please let me in." I would speak in a moderate voice because we lived in an apartment and I did not want the next door neighbor to hear me. I would go to our bedroom window and kitchen window and speak softly. After asking and begging three to four times, he would let me in and I would get cussed at; he would complain about my hair being messed up—that is what he would call it—because praising God, dancing before the Lord, my hair would get out of place a little. Again, I say I didn't mind what I would encounter at that time, but the Mothers wanted me to be subject to my husband; therefore, a couple of them would send me word or point to me to go home and I would obey them and leave to go home to make my curfew.

On many occasions, whoever dropped me off home, on my way, I would ask them to pray with me that the night latch wouldn't be on the door and if it was, they would wait in the car and not leave me by myself until I got inside. They would encourage me and lift me up where I could go on. Before the night would be over, my husband would pull the cover from off of me and say to me, "You think you are going to come in here and snore in my face after you done wallowed all over the floor?

See, you must know back in the day, we would call Jesus at the altar until sometimes we would fall out on the floor and the Spirit of God would be dealing with us and sometimes we would get to rolling and that's where we got the name—Holy Roller. So, he did not want me to be out there 'holy rolling' although he was doing everything he felt to do that was wrong. Still, I presented myself as a wife to him; not holding back my due benevolence to him; I did not hold back in cooking for him nor performing my wifely duties such as washing his clothes, keeping his house clean, and attending to his children. At this time in my life, we had four children together.

PRAYER AROUND THE COMMODE

I remember during the week nights, we would have Bible Study on Tuesday night. Well, Tuesday was fast day also for the church. So, every Tuesday and Friday were fast days. I mainly had to fast those days asking the Lord to let him let me go to church tonight. I would fast and pray and believe God for going to church. For the devil of it, my husband did not want me going to church on those nights. He said he wanted the Ol' Pearl back because I had changed so drastically and he could not stand nor understand the anointing that was on my life.

One night, I came home and when he did let me in, I was so lifted where I would go to sleep peaceful and he would snatch the cover and push me out of the bed, but I was as humble as a lamb. Therefore, I would go on to the living room and carry my cover and lie on the sofa. Well, that would anger him and he would come and pull the cover from off of me there too. So, this particular night, instead of sitting up until he told me to come on to bed or until I felt it was safe for me to go and get back in the bed, I decided to go and shut up in the bathroom to fall down on my knees at the commode. With the lid down, I went into my heavenly language. He did not understand that language and he would be begging and knocking on the door asking me to please stop; he won't do it anymore, but I felt led to continue and he got a case knife from the kitchen drawer and forced the door open asking and pulling me up from the floor begging me to stop speaking in tongues. That was a scare for him that night, but he couldn't hold out to his promise; he harassed me other times about going to church and being out there making a fool out of myself was his perception. Really, he couldn't' understand the spiritual part of my life. I did not shut him out of my life, yet I served him as my husband.

Because of things I was suffering, I kept myself in prayer.

Day	Time	Service
Tuesday	Morning	Prayer
Thursday	Noon	Prayer
Friday	Evenings	Prayer and Tarry

I also attended prayer revivals, thanksgiving prayer service, and church revivals. I was faithful and I did not kick against the brick. I came under submission to God's word. Two of my favorite songs in that trying time in my life were "The Word of God Brought Me Here" and "Run, Don't Look Back." There was running in the feet of my heart and a mind to do right whatever the cost.

Another one of my favorite songs was "If It Cost My Life, I've Got to Make It to That City." I was taught, according to the word of the Lord, that it would cost me everything. Leaving all to follow the Jesus walk would cost me everything—even my life. The Apostle Peter makes this clear in Luke 18:28-30.

> Then Peter said, Lo, we have left all, and followed thee. And he said unto them, Verily I say unto you, There is no man that hath left house, or parents, or brethren, or wife, or children, for the kingdom of God's sake, Who shall not receive manifold more in this present time, and in the world to come life everlasting.
>
> –Luke 18:28-30

If any man come to me, and hate not his father, and mother, and wife, and children, and brethren, and sisters, yea, and his own life also, he cannot be my disciple. And whosoever doth not bear his cross, and come after me, cannot be my disciple.

–Luke 14:26-27

What I understood from these scriptures is that my trials were coming through my marriage. I had a cross to bear, so I picked up my cross and followed Jesus by not letting anything or anyone come before my Lord. I put Him first in my life.

CHAPTER FIVE

MY MISCARRIAGE

I was taught by some of the Mothers in the church to have children and try not to prevent them, so I did. I did not like having those children. I was going through so much in the marriage and I was under so much stress. However, I wanted to do everything that I felt would please the Lord. I got pregnant with my fifth child. I became so sick and weak that I hardly had strength to get out of the bed. I was going through much hardship in my marriage. My husband was going out every week at night by himself. I would lie in bed feeling very troubled because I could discern that he was out doing wrong. One day, I became so ill with a headache. My mother lived next door and learned that I was sick with this terrible headache. Well, a lady down the street visited my mother and my mother revealed to her that I had a headache. So, she and my mother came over and the lady wanted to pray for me. Well, I did not believe in this woman because I was told she was a fortune telling lady and I knew the truth. I was being raised in holiness, so as this woman began to pray, she tied knots in a string, which was her belief, but not mine. As she put that string around my head and snapped her fingers, I dismissed the little ritual out from harming me and believed in my Lord and Savior Jesus Christ. My husband either hadn't gotten home from work or was out on his house visits. In looking to the Lord for my help, I did end up feeling better.

What was going on, I was under such an attack from the adversary, the devil. I was hurting over my life situation in my marriage. I would cry at night because I would be afraid of being home by myself alone plus my husband was out in the streets doing things that were against me and our marriage. He would come home late at night with no words or an explanation. I took that week after week for a while. I was used to going to Tuesday prayer meeting, so I wanted to go to the morning prayer at 10:00, but I had not been able to because of the attack that was upon my body with all the weakness and feeling sick by being pregnant. I would be sick during the whole pregnancy—sick to the stomach vomiting and spitting.

However, on this particular Tuesday morning, I pulled myself up to go to prayer and I had to walk to prayer, which was not too far. I walked to prayer that morning being with child around two months. At prayer, there were not many of us there and someone was on the altar seeking God for soul salvation. This person had a little child and I held the little child while the other saints were praying with the individual and all of a sudden, blood began to run from me and I got one of the missionaries' attention and asked her to take me home and she did. As I entered in my house, I went to the bathroom and more blood was coming. I cleaned up and went to lie down. The next day, I called the hospital and they told me to come in. I went and was kept overnight. A dilation and curettage, known as a D & C, was performed by scraping my womb to remove tissue from inside my uterus to remove the heavy bleeding to clean the uterine lining after a miscarriage. The next evening, I was dismissed.

By the time I got home, I went to bed and all of a sudden, my nerves were on edge where I could not bear to hear anyone's footsteps in the house. My mother, husband, another neighbor, and a niece were there with me. Someone was in the kitchen handling pots and talking. They were trying to do a good deed by cooking for me, but I could not bear to hear their voices and footsteps and the rattling of the lids from the pots. I was living in a small apartment. I called for my niece and asked her to call some of the saints from the church and tell them to pray for me and they did. As I was speaking to my niece, I felt like I was about to have a nervous breakdown for I could not stand to hear my own voice. It was heart wrenching for me to talk. I could not even pray for myself. I felt like I would lose it just by thinking, so I shut down my mind and just laid there waiting for the Lord to touch me and He did immediately. I am so thankful for His healing touch.

The result of that encounter was that I had begun to miscarry at the church. Now, I know it doesn't sound right to miscarry a baby and you are in church in prayer service. Well, I see it like this. The prayer service did not cause my miscarriage. My body was already broken down from stress and mistreatment and I learned from medical knowledge that anytime there is a miscarriage, it is for the best because if not, the baby would be abnormal. Miscarriages mostly are caused by a one off fault in the genes (a genetic defect) and why it happened like it did only God knows.

I got over that episode of losing my baby to go on with life in Christ. While living in the apartment next door to my mom with four children, we were knitted together. I taught my children about the love of Jesus bringing them up in the admonition of the Lord. They were very active in church, the children's choir, children's church, and as they matured, they went on to young people's ministry. We all were very dedicated. We hardly missed any major services because I loved the Lord and was training my children up in the Lord. They weren't angels, but they were good little children. I remember my mother, who was a wonderful woman, loved and respected by many, was not saved and filled with the Holy Ghost. Her dedication was to go to church once a month for communion, but to send us every Sunday as children. She was not in the knowledge of sanctification and being Holy Ghost filled, but she lived a good and moral life; however, I prayed and fasted for my mother to come in the knowledge of more of the Lord knowing Him in a more perfect (mature) way. One Saturday morning, I felt led to fast all day for my mother to be saved and filled with the Holy Ghost and that next Tuesday, I asked her to go with me to morning prayer at 10:00 and she agreed to, which was unusual because she thought that kind of life was for certain people. My mother went to the altar and called on the name of Jesus for soul salvation and God heard her cry and delivered her soul that day. That Sunday, she went back to the church and continued on the altar to be filled with the Holy Ghost. The Lord overshadowed her with His presence and she was made glad and she left there highly blessed. She came back the next Tuesday morning and she was now filled with the Holy Ghost and she became one of them baptized believers! Amen.

She was more beautiful and wonderful after her Pentecostal experience. I remember before she had her Pentecostal experiences, my oldest little boy would come home from church and we would stop by mama's house before going home. One Sunday, he said to his Grandmama, "Grandmama you can't join in. You must be born in." That pierced her heart and she gave much thought to this little saying, but he was really witnessing to her. From that experience, we went to church together. She became a greater mother in the Lord. I was happy that my mother had received Christ in a very personal way. My children and other family members—we all went on serving the Lord in the beauty of Holiness.

My husband came home one day wanting to get a better job as a City Bus Driver. He made his request known to me and I made it known to the Lord; with prayer and faith, the Lord granted his request. He made more money with benefits and we were faring better than we had been. However, he had so much exposure with the public where he could not handle the temptation. He became promiscuous by having many sexual relationships. His attitude had changed towards me; he had no time for me and he was constantly going off staying for a while on weekends and weekdays. He had too many interests on the outside and I knew by the Holy Spirit, but I never stopped doing what I was to do as a wife.

There was even a time he asked me to go to the clinic to be treated for a sexual disease. I was so hurt and embarrassed. I knew I needed to go because his treatment was not enough. I needed to be treated too. I was embarrassed of the fact that I was a woman of God who was true to her husband, but he had given me a sexual disease. Secondly, I did not want anyone to see me going into such a clinic. I did not know who I was going to see when I walked into the clinic. Nevertheless, I prepared myself to go. When I got there, I became so ashamed until I could not go in. I left, looking up to God, telling God to take care of me and I went back home. During that time, I still cooked his food and carried it to him. He loved to eat in his bedroom because most of the time, the next thing he would do was go to bed and rest, so he could get up and go out later. That was then when I began to say, "When I should have treated him like a dog, I treated him like a king."

Those are some of the days that I fixed his favorite dinner and served it to him on a tray and carried it to him in the living room or bedroom or whatever room he chose. I would fix him a T-bone steak, baked potato, and okra, which was considered one of his favorite dishes—with a tossed salad made up of fresh vegetables, and as I said on *Brian Carn Live (Daystar)*, I would cut that potato down to the middle, cut it across, and push it up and drop the butter, salt, and pepper in it to make it look interesting. Then a little later, I would ask my husband if I could go to church that night and most times, if I have served him a good meal and got the house cleaned and was prayed up and had fasted for the day, I would get a chance to go to Bible Study and Friday night prayer and tarry service. I did not have the freedom to go to regular church services or revivals. I had to pray and fast to go. My husband would bring a couple of beers home and place them in the refrigerator and I used to serve it with his dinner because that's what he wanted, but after I got saved I would not serve him beer. I let him know I was saved now, so I couldn't serve him beer and the Lord had him to be calm about it.

I was so pleased about his calm spirit. I began to pray and ask God to bless us with a home and he did. When we first started out looking for a nice house, it was not easy. We were turned down because our credit was not too good. My husband had lied to me when he first met me and said that he had plenty of money and nothing to do with it, so I bought into that and did not know his credit status until I married him. When I started trying to get furniture, I realized he had poor credit, but the Lord blessed us. Where some turned us down for credit or offered a less than desirable home I did not like in a less than desirable neighborhood where I did not want to live, God blessed us. Because I was desperate for a home for our children, I was about to take what I was not happy with, but then my faith came alive in a more excellent way, so we did not accept what was being offered to us. I came back, prayed, and believed God the more and when we went back out, God led us to the right place with the right information. We were offered a brand new brick home with four bedrooms, two baths, in a nice neighborhood. We had the opportunity to have the house built by picking out all the materials from the bricks, even the lot, and everything else that goes with the house. To God be the glory!

My husband could not see us moving up that much. He felt he could not pay that much for the house, but I encouraged him to let him know our God was able and faithful to us. Our house was built. We moved in. Our house was beautiful and new and I had decorated it. I had the house blessed and prayed over.

After moving in the house, I recognized that my husband's oldest son lived around the corner with his mother and he saw us moving in. He was standing across the street looking over at us and I recognized him and invited him to come over. From that day to now, he has been my child also. I am mama to him; he was only around 11 years old at that time I suppose. He loves me and I love him and treat him as a son. We have a mother-son relationship. Later on, I came into the knowledge that my husband's first wife lived on the same street we lived on one block from us. With the Lord on my side is how I survived 55 years of marriage with an adulterous husband. I allowed God to be Lord of my life.

Remember, my husband was a bus driver—a City Bus Driver. Now, he wasn't only driving the bus, but he was also courting hard with the women. He liked the young ladies too. One of my sons had a beef with his father for the mere fact that my son would see a young lady, try and get with her, and he would find out that his daddy had been trying to hit on that same young lady. This became a problem in our home where my son became very angry with his dad; he was hearing too much about his dad out there in the streets.

CHAPTER SIX

CALLED INTO MINISTRY

My worship was for real; that is how I survived 55 years of marriage with my adulterous husband. After being saved for six years, the Lord called me into ministry as a preacher of the gospel, but in my church, you were not called a preacher, but a missionary, so I heard the Lord clearly when He called me to preach His word. I was so afraid to tell my husband, but one day, God gave me the boldness to let him know that I was called into the ministry to preach His word. My husband took it well to my surprise. He replied back to me for me to do what the Lord says. I did not know why he took it so well, but I knew the Lord had His hand in it. What I did not know was he was going with a woman who was in the same kind of church I was in, which was a Pentecostal Church. I didn't know it at the time, but I found out later.

After the Lord called me into the ministry, it seems as though my trials in my marriage got worse. I still wasn't all the way free to go to church like I wished. My husband did begin to let me go, but he wanted to withhold his car from me, so I had to ask him to use the car to go to church and he would say no. I began to pray and fast when we had revivals going on or regular services. I learned to pray all during the day asking the Lord to let him let me have the car for church on those nights.

There was a period of time when I had to go through that so I knew the routine thing that I would do. I would go first as humbly as I could asking for the car keys to use the car to go to church. For the devil of it, he would say no. I would go back and look up to God and say, “Lord, I believe you for those keys.” I would go back to my husband asking for the keys and the answer would be no again. I would not give up. I would send my children one by one telling them to go and ask their daddy if we could use the car to go to church. See, I would have the children and myself already dressed, so once those keys were released, we could jump in the car and go on to church. They had to go one by one and say, "Daddy, mama say can we have the key to the car so we can go to church?" No, no, no, would be the answer for all of us, but we knew how to use our faith to get a yes. We would all go and sit and wait until my husband would call out to one of the children and say, "Carry these keys to your mama." That's all we wanted to hear and out the door we would go, but my, my, we begged for those keys.

There were times he was so mean and wouldn't give up the car to me and I would have to walk to the bus stop and catch the bus to church. I would then get a ride back with someone from the church or I would call around and get a ride with a church member there and back. I had a season of that kind of treatment.

One Tuesday night, I was getting a ride home from Bible Study and the sister that I was in the car with had to carry another lady to this particular apartment complex. As we were going in, my husband was coming out. I saw him at my surprise. I was so shocked where I wouldn't say anything to anyone in the car. I kept quiet and by the time I got home, he was home like he had been there all the time. To make sure that was him that I had just seen, I touched his car to see if the engine was hot and it was. He was in the bed under the covers.

A few weeks later, I was home on a Saturday. The children and I were cleaning up, washing clothes, and I had Sunday's dinner cooking, so when we got home on Sunday, our food would already be done. I was working a weekday job and that's why we had so much to do on Saturdays. My husband had not a mind to help me with things of that nature—cooking and cleaning and tending to the children. He saw to the yards and cars with the boys' help. While he was out on his regular schedule doing what he does, I got a call from him and he said to me “I'm going to the dog track with a guy.” I replied and asked, "Where are you?" That he did not like for me to do. He rebuked me and hung up the phone, so I decided to stop what I was doing and go see if he was at that apartment complex where I saw him coming out before. Don’t you know his car was parked right there? I knocked on about three doors asking for him. At the third door, children answered.

I asked for him and they said no he was not there, so I went to my car and decided to wait for him there. It was not 25 minutes before he came up in a car with a man. I asked him, “Why is your car here? He said, “I'm here with some friends.” I said, “Let me meet them.” He said, “No I'm going home.” He would not carry me to meet these so-called friends he had out there in this apartment complex. He claimed he was coming back from the dog track. All of that was a lie.

I went back home with no satisfaction—nothing, but lies. That was not my normal character to go and look for him, but I just felt led that particular day after he had hung up the phone on me like he had done so many other times. Yet, he never cleared up this incident.

Later on in my marriage, I started getting phone calls and the person on the other end would not say anything. I decided to pray and ask God to make that person talk and the person listened to me through the whole prayer. In about 30 minutes or less, the person called back and began telling me a lot of what was going on between her mother and my husband. She gave me information about the day my husband told me he went to the dog track, but was laid up in some woman’s apartment. The person on the phone informed me that when I came to that apartment that day, my husband was there. She gave me the name, location, and floor of her mother’s job.

Please understand, I was not a violent woman, but I did go to the department store to see how this woman looked, which was all I wanted to see. She came and asked me, "Can I help you?" I said, "No." I then left. When I got home, I told my husband about my encounter I had that day and that I had been to see this lady. He said, "I know." "How?" I asked. "She told me. She knows you. People know you Pearl. They know my car. They see you in my car driving."

Since she knew me, I thought I would call her and ask her how long she and my husband had been together. I did and she shocked me. She told me they had been together for 10 years. I was very hurt. I went to the Holy Bible, prayer meetings, and good spiritual services to stay strong. He came home later to lie to me and tell me that it didn't mean anything to him. Yet, they had a 10-year relationship. How could a 10-year relationship not mean anything to the persons involved?

I would come home some nights from church and during the 80s and 90s, we had some phones with the cords hanging from them. I would walk in the room and find a phone cord still swinging from the phone being hung up fast.

One of our daughters told me her daddy would bring her fast food snacks to keep her from telling on him when she would find him on the phone or whatever. She loved to eat. I will never forget my husband heard me speaking to a prayer partner about his wrongdoings and he got angry. He walked up to me and slapped me and walked away. I turned to the Lord for help and he carried me to this passage of scripture—2 Corinthians 12:9. "And he said unto me, My grace is sufficient for thee: for my strength is made perfect in weakness." I began to lean on the strength of the Lord. Reading that scripture caused me to stop crying and look up. My husband left home that evening and returned later with no words.

CHAPTER SEVEN

WHY I TOOK SO MUCH

I believed the scripture and wanted to see manifestation for my marriage. I wanted to see the scripture fulfilled where it says in 1 Corinthians 7:13-14.

And the woman which hath an husband that believeth not, and if he be pleased to dwell with her, let her not leave him. For the unbelieving husband is sanctified by the wife, and the unbelieving wife is sanctified by the husband: else were your children unclean; but now are they holy.

–1 Corinthians 7:13-14

He was committing adultery. I could have divorced him, but I chose not.

My heart's desire was to see my husband saved. God had his hand on me from my birth to be this missionary that I so desired to be from a child. One thing the Holy Spirit revealed and put in my spirit is that I cannot go and save others and never have started at home. Jesus told the disciples in Acts 1:8,

But ye shall receive power, after that the Holy Ghost is come upon you: and ye shall be witnesses unto me both in Jerusalem, and in all Judaea, and in Samaria, and unto the uttermost part of the earth.

–Acts 1:8

JERUSALEM WAS THE JESUS HOME BASE.

And, being assembled together with them, commanded them that they should not depart from Jerusalem, but wait for the promise of the Father, which, saith he, ye have heard of me.

–Acts 1:4

My conviction was before starting my ministry abroad, I had to make sure I started at home. I had to love my husband and children to life. The same conviction is given unto you. Women, you cannot minister to the world and neglect your family and husband.

My conviction was to love my husband to life. Why look for another? I had to wait for him to be resurrected. I waited on the Lord and He heard my cry and brought me out of my pain and hurt. I knew pain and hurt every day and night. All night pain, all day pain, going to bed with pain, driving with pain, going to work with pain, all alone with pain, until it took my strength, but not my will. I had a mind to live right and stay up under the blood until Jesus showed up in my marriage. Not my will, but His will be done.

I know what it is to get up out of the bed at the 11 o'clock hour and begin to drive going nowhere special, but just had to get out from under the pressure. I would just be driving on the freeway, praying, crying, and hurting. My husband cared not; he would be sleeping while I would be under attack concerning our marriage. I would go to bed with my face tied up because of pain in my heart and spirit, but I would refer to the scripture where Jesus told Paul in 2 Corinthians 12:9, my grace is sufficient. My strength is perfect in your weakness. He did not promise to take this thing from him, but He promised Paul grace and His strength to endure. Paul answered stating

> Most gladly therefore will I rather glory in my infirmities, that the power of Christ may rest upon me.
>
> –2 Corinthians 12:9

Surely, the anointing was upon my life heavily. I found out also that the greater my trial was, the heavier my anointing was. God's power rested upon me. I too began to glory in my affliction by giving God glory, honor, and praise. I had a praise in my mouth, a clap in my hand, and a dance in my feet. I kept my praise hot.

I remember I was pregnant in this particular season of my life and I visited a certain church. I was going through rough mountains in my marriage and I struck out in a dance. By my being pregnant, the usher or someone tried to grab hold of me, but the Holy Ghost power of God was too quick and fast for the flesh man. So I was gone, dancing on one feet, and when the usher reached out for me, she could not stop me for I was in the spirit.

That's how I survived 55 years of marriage with an adulterous husband. I kept myself under the umbrella of the anointing by praising God and worshipping God daily. Reading the word of God daily and most of all humbling myself under the mighty hand of God, that he may exalt me in due time—1 Peter 5:6; there is always a due time with God—Galatians 6:9; and let us not be weary in well doing for in due season (the proper season) we shall reap if we faint not.

We are to do good to others and God will be glorified. You shall reap a great harvest if you glorify God by doing good. Back to 1 Peter 5:5—we are to be subject to one another and be clothed with humility; for God resisted the proud and giveth grace to the humble. I believe the word giveth means to continue to flow. I am a living witness that you don't lose by obeying God in His word.

I survived 55 years of marriage by doing what Peter said in 1 Peter 5:7—casting all my cares upon the Lord; for he cares for me. My spirit would say, “Yes, Lord” to His Word.

I found the word to fit my situation. 1 Peter 5:8 says be sober (serious), be vigilant (watchful, wide-awake, and alert), never be off your guard. Be ready every moment to resist the devil because your adversary, the devil, as a roaring lion, walketh about, seeking whom he may devour: v.10, the God of all grace, who hath called us until his eternal glory by Christ Jesus. After that ye have suffered a while make you perfect, which means mature, stablish, which means establish you in the faith and strengthen, meaning spiritual strength, settle you, meaning to be grounded in the faith; having a good foundation, but not until you have suffered a while.

I decided since my marriage is being tried I may as well let God do some finish work in me.

Being confident of this very thing, that he which hath begun a good work in you will perform it until the day of Jesus Christ:

– Philippians 1:6

For ye have need of patience, that, after ye have done the will of God, ye might receive the promise.

(Eternal life with Christ)

– Hebrews 10:36

My brethren, count it all joy when ye fall into divers temptations; Knowing this, that the trying of your faith worketh patience. But let patience have her perfect work, that ye may be perfect and entire, wanting nothing.

– James 1:2-4

James speaks of the testing of the Christians. My brethren, count it all joy when you fall into (be caught by) divers temptations, (different trials) knowing this that the trying of your faith worketh patience, but let patience have her perfect work that ye may be perfect (mature) and entire (complete) wanting nothing.

In Romans 5:3, I began to realize that when we are being tried we must learn to glory in tribulations also according to Paul and the other apostles, knowing that tribulation is working the patience and patience working experience and experience working hope: these scriptures showed me myself.

Through my trials, I began to have my eyes enlightened through God's word knowing that tribulation worketh patience, experience, and hope; therefore, I realized I was not going through this for nothing. I knew I was coming out like pure gold. I was going through to come out; to be an overcomer that I may be a witness of God's miraculous power; that I may witness to other married couples. I was like jewels in the making, His special treasure, a treasure made up of costly things such as gold and diamonds and rubies.

And they shall be mine, saith the LORD of hosts, in that day when I make up my jewels; and I will spare them, as a man spareth his own son that serveth him.

– Malachi 3:17

I began to realize that I was a part of His jewels. Now remember, we who have a call of ministry for our life have been given much and much is required of us. One day, I was home seeking God, having my devotion and the Holy Spirit spoke to me in a gentle fashion and commissioned me to go and do ministry in homes, to carry the gospel and healing ministry to the sick and shut in. The Spirit of God led me to my front door and spoke to my spirit and said go. It was so powerful that I immediately called my pastor to let him know what God had spoken. My pastor gave his approval and I immediately started going into homes praying for the sick and having devotion with them and God healed, encouraged, and set free during those prayers. The ministry was enlarged with workers. We went into many homes down through the years and street services, churches with revival services, nursing homes, and prisons.

One evening, my husband would not let me use the car to go do a house service. That was when I first was getting started and the sister who was going with me to a young lady's apartment had no transportation either. We caught the same bus and prayed for the young lady, sang, and preached the word. Before service was over, another faithful sister came and a few others and we blessed that home and God had transportation waiting for us to carry us home. No matter how the devil used my husband, God always had a ram in the bush. We left there rejoicing in the Lord.

I was determined not to let anything separate me from His love or anyone.

Who shall separate us from the love of Christ? Shall tribulation, or distress, or persecution, or famine, or nakedness, or peril, or sword?
– Romans 8:35

I was persuaded that nothing would stop me. Satan, through my husband, tried to stop me by making things hard for me, but I did not stop. I kept on keeping on.

One night, I was asked to go into a home and have services with a young lady who had cancer. It was on a cold night which was my regular ministry night, but my husband would not keep our baby that night. We had a baby boy, our last child, who was an arm baby at the time. My husband let me know he was not keeping the baby to look after him when I'm gone. He said for me to take the baby with me. I wrapped my baby up in a blanket, dressed him warmly, and carried him to the house service with me and laid him in a bed. As he slept, we went on doing the Lord's work. My baby slept good while we were singing and praying and God healed that lady from cancer and she lives today. God can use you during your storm, your valley experiences, and raise you up to a mountain dew refreshing anointing.

God called me to be busy for him during my greatest time of trial. I kept busy for the Lord and as my suffering became intense, my ministry would grow and glow. God would meet us every time, whether it was at the street service, house service, church service, prison or nursing home, God moved by His power. House services would be packed out and everybody would leave refreshed. Many homes were blessed by our showing up.

I was doing a Wednesday night house service this particular night, at one of my husband's niece's houses, when my husband decided to come and get me from service. He knew well I was in charge of the service that night. By the time Satan put in his heart to come get me, the Lord was through doing what we had asked him to do and that was to fill a young man with the Holy Ghost and to bless the house where we were. Well, the Lord had finished the assignment. As I was giving closing remarks, I heard my husband's tires coming around the curves in the sub-division we were in and I immediately sensed there was trouble. I humbled myself and went outside to see what he wanted and he ordered me in the car. I asked him to let me go back in and let the others know that I had to leave. I did. I also asked one of the sisters to close out the service and for them to pray for me because I was a little frightened because my husband had never come and gotten me from a house service.

I did not have my own car that night, so I had to get in the car with him and he was driving wild like a mad man. While he was driving like he was intoxicated, I was praying and I offered myself up to God that night saying, Lord if it's for me to die tonight, just let my soul be right and take care of my children.

"Lord if it's for me to die tonight, just let my soul be right and take care of my children."

After arriving home, he opened the trunk of the car and he reached his hand in it to get something out of the trunk. I'm standing there looking at a knife in the trunk; a large kitchen knife and I'm thinking, Oh my Lord! Am I going to die? By that time, he closed the trunk and walked in the house. Later, I followed behind him wondering how far to go and were the children all right because he had gone to the back bedroom and I was out front in the living and dining room. I was fearful to go on back in the hall entrance to the bedroom. I prayed and got my faith to rise where I went on back to the bedroom to see whether the children were all right and they were. However, my not knowing what my husband was doing, I finally looked to see what he was doing and he was in the bed going to sleep. God had tamed that lion! Whatever Satan had put in my husband's mind to do that night, God intercepted it; He raised up a standard against the enemy and caused a sleep to fall upon my husband.

The day came where his father passed and he did not have a dark blue suit, so he went alone to purchase one. He came home with this very nice suit for his father's funeral. I looked at the suit and said, "My, this is a nice suit." Well, I had no problem with the suit being nice because I like nice things. The fact I was after was who picked out this suit? He did not pick this suit for the reason it did not look like his taste or money. (Smiling) Anyway, I let it pass. I will tell you about that suit in a later chapter—wait for it! So much happened in my life to try and stop me, but I was sold out and persuaded.

For I am persuaded, that neither death, nor life, nor angels, nor principalities, nor powers, nor things present, nor things to come, Nor height, nor depth, nor any other creature, shall be able to separate us from the love of God, which is in Christ Jesus our Lord.

– Romans 8:38-39

One day I left early from my job to go to a doctor's appointment for I was not feeling well. I was struggling and fighting with all of those spirits belonging to my husband. After leaving the doctor's office, I was minding my business driving home. Coming down a certain street to get home, I looked to my left and as I approached that certain street, I thought I saw my husband's car parked out on the road where some apartments were, but I kept driving and went on home. Now, I knew it was my husband's car. Because mostly all of my husband's cars were somewhat different with a uniqueness about them. When he came home, I asked him why he was at those apartments with his car being parked on the side of them. He said he had stopped to see someone. Later on, I found out that was one of his girlfriend's places, but I kept giving myself over to the Lord and loving him.

I would ask God to take the hurt from out of the hurt; in other words, I hurt so much, that whatever I had to suffer, I did not want to feel the hurt. I wanted to become emotionally numb to the hurt I was experiencing in my marriage. I can recall driving to church with the children when they were around 15 or 16 years of age. As I was driving, that old devil attacked my nerves and I lost the ability to drive. The enemy came against me, but he could never possess me. I always remember Psalm 34:19,

Many are the afflictions of the righteous: but the LORD delivereth him out of them all.

–Psalm 34:19

There were quite a few downfalls, but I was still in the hands of God.

I felt bad finding out that apartment complex was one of his stomping grounds and where one of his girlfriends lived. God's grace was sufficient for me and when I would become so weak, His strength was perfect and I was able to lean on his strength. I was still in the hands of God.

Cell phones were not invented during this season of my husband's infidelity; therefore, he had to use a payphone. He became almost a payphone king. He was found being seen in the payphone booth so often a lot of times it would be reported to me by a friend or relative unintentionally and intentionally. God did not let too much be hidden from me for He knew my enablement.

I kept doing ministry and carrying my cross, which was not a small one. It was indeed a large cross that was heavy to bear. I had a radio program weekly called "The Love of God and Healing Touch Ministry." I was faithful to that call for a few years and people were blessed. I had people to tell me they were still hearing me on the radio even when I was off at the time.

One day, my husband said unto me, "I want to have another child before I become forty years old." I thought he was out of his mind. I didn't want any more children for I would be so sick the whole nine months and so rejected from my husband during that time. I would go to the valley of loneliness, despair, and forsakenness; however, I kept my faith in Jesus Christ and stayed faithful to him and I did have that child; our fifth child and sixth pregnancy. One of my favorite scriptures was 1 Peter 4:1-2.

Forasmuch then as Christ hath suffered for us in the flesh, arm yourselves likewise with the same mind: for he that hath suffered in the flesh hath ceased from sin; that he no longer should live the rest of his time in the flesh to the lusts of men but to the will of God.

–1 Peter 4:1-2

Beloved, think it not strange concerning the fiery trial which is to try you, as though some strange thing happened unto you: But rejoice, inasmuch as ye are partakers of Christ's sufferings; that, when his glory shall be revealed, ye may be glad also with exceeding joy.

–1 Peter 4:12-13

Scriptures of this nature helped me to go on to my destiny. I took Paul's instructions on how to be strong in the Lord.

Finally, my brethren, be strong in the Lord, and in the power of his might.[11] Put on the whole armour of God, that ye may be able to stand against the wiles of the devil. For we wrestle not against flesh and blood, but against principalities, against powers, against the rulers of the darkness of this world, against spiritual wickedness in high places.

– Ephesians 6:10-12

In my marriage, I had to put on the whole armor of God and keep it on.

Wherefore take unto you the whole armour of God, that ye may be able to withstand in the evil day, and having done all, to stand. Stand therefore, having your loins girt about with truth, and having on the breastplate of righteousness;

And your feet shod with the preparation of the gospel of peace; Above all, taking the shield of faith, wherewith ye shall be able to quench all the fiery darts of the wicked. And take the helmet of salvation, and the sword of the Spirit, which is the word of God: Praying always with all prayer and supplication in the Spirit, and watching thereunto with all perseverance and supplication for all saints;

– Ephesians 6:13-18

I applied these verses of scripture to my personal life and pulled life from them, which sustained me. I needed the scriptures in my life. I was called into the ministry, and carrying my fifth child, I delivered my message. I went through hard trials and rejection, but I was faithful as a wife unto my husband whether he was a true husband to me. I was a young woman who studied God's word and God's word says in 1 Corinthians 7:5, that married couples are to be faithful to each other always—and yes, this includes in the bedroom.

Defraud ye not one the other, except it be with consent for a time, that ye may give yourselves to fasting and prayer; and come together again, that Satan tempt you not for your incontinency.

–1 Corinthians 7:5

The wife hath not power of her own body, but the husband: and likewise also the husband hath not power of his own body, but the wife.

–1 Corinthians 7:4

And unto the married I command, yet not I, but the Lord, Let not the wife depart from her husband:

–1 Corinthians 7:10

I cherished the word of God. My ultimate goal was to please the Lord.

Again, when my husband should have been treated like a dog, I treated him like a king. My being called into the ministry of pastoring was a big day because the Lord had tamed my husband's spirit somewhat. So, I was able to do Wednesday nights in the den of the house for a year. My husband parked the cars for me in the backyard and made sure everyone who attended was parked properly down the streets. Looks like I ministered and had my babies.

My babies were all born before I started pastoring. My sixth child was born the next year, which was 1973 and my seventh child in 1975. Believe me, when I was having those last babies, the devil wanted me to throw in the towel, but my hope was built on nothing less than Jesus' blood and righteousness.

CHAPTER EIGHT
THE ROLLER COASTER

My life became like a roller coaster. It went from one episode to another. The trials kept on rolling. 2 Corinthians 4:8-9,

We are troubled on every side, yet not distressed; we are perplexed, but not in despair; Persecuted, but not forsaken; cast down, but not destroyed;

–2 Corinthians 4:8-9

There was a time in my life where I was troubled on every side, distressed, perplexed, forsaken cast down, but not destroyed. I would sit at home and do my chores, but not have the will to take my gown off nor my night scarf. I was very weak in my body and my mind was overloaded from all the works of the enemy against our marriage.

One thing is for sure—out of all I encountered, I never lost my joy. I never lost my praise. I remember my husband would go out at night never to take me with him and I knew he would be out with his woman. I would train myself to make sure I would pray for him and the woman. At first, it was hard to pray for their souls, but I kept on praying until I felt it in my soul where I was able to pray from my heart and pray that they both would be saved.

My husband would come in some nights after being out and fall on his knees. I would be so happy because I had prayed for soul salvation for him and whomever he was with, but I believe, at some point, he began to pretend he was praying. I think he was doing it to fool me hoping I would not say anything to him. You better know that God had his time to move on my husband. My prayers were full of faith.

I had so many different experiences relating to my marriage. This is why I can write to you and encourage you to wait on the Lord and see Him work. Again one of my favorite scriptures that kept my heart lifted comes from the book of Hebrews.

Cast not away therefore your confidence, which hath great recompence of reward. For ye have need of patience, that, after ye have done the will of God, ye might receive the promise. For yet a little while, and he that shall come will come, and will not tarry. Now the just shall live by faith: but if any man draw back, my soul shall have no pleasure in him. But we are not of them who draw back unto perdition; but of them that believe to the saving of the soul.

– Hebrews 10:35-39

Scriptures of this nature and the praying and encouraging mothers of the church are what kept me during these difficult moments. Once again, I will never forget the day I was trodden down in my spirit and feeling sorry for myself with a broken heart with tears rolling. A knock suddenly came to my door. I answered it and it was one of the mothers of the church and she felt led to come by and have prayer with me; her visit and prayer blessed my heart so much. It was just like God had come to visit me. When you give all of yourself to the Lord, He truly will be faithful to you. That was an experience of my being weak and sorrowful, but God's grace was sufficient for me and His strength made me strong. I felt like an angel had visited me that day.

I began to grow in God and the more I grew, the more the Lord revealed to me how to love my husband in spite of him. I saw where he needed help and that the devil had attacked our marriage and it was in trouble. I had to realize that I was the one who was saved and had the Holy Ghost power. My husband was not and he was powerless; he was no match for the devil.

CHAPTER NINE

THE WEAPONS OF OUR WARFARE

The weapons of our warfare are not carnal and God used the power of dreams to remind me of this. I had a dream one night where a large snake was wrapped around my husband's neck and he was not fighting much at all at the snake to try and get himself loose. I was wondering why because in the natural, my husband would fight. In the dream, he was only hitting at the snake, but not to pull that snake from around his neck. Also, in the dream, a large snake was around my neck and I could not understand why a snake would be around MY neck. I began to look to my husband for help and he was not helping me, which was also odd. One thing about my husband is he would always see about me; he didn't want anyone else to harm me. He would get upset about it. Every now and then, he would hit at the snake that was around me. I began fighting the snake off of me and I then awoke from the dream. I asked the Lord,

"What did that dream mean?" I got no answer until around a few months later. The dream opened up to me. God revealed to me that the reason my husband was not fighting the snake off of him was because he was powerless. That's the reason he could not help me. He had no power against the enemy—the devil. The reason I was able to fight the demon off of me, which was in the form of a snake, is because I had power in the Holy Ghost.

There, he was able to show me where I had the weapon of mass destruction. My husband in his flesh was no match for the adversary, the devil, who had come to destroy our marriage. I saw the picture clearer; I saw where my husband needed my help. He was in bondage.

I could not, however, understand why the snake was around me too. Well, the revelation to that is that the devil had come in against our marriage to take both of us out and I'm having to fight for us both. My husband had no power in the Holy Ghost and was no match for the devil.

I began to see more clearly. It was not my husband, but it was the devil, the adversary, that opposed what God had ordained and many times, there are generational curses that have to be broken. Many times, they're acting out what is in their bloodline. I used to preach the message "Can God Consider You?

> And the LORD said unto Satan, Hast thou considered my servant Job, that there is none like him in the earth, a perfect and an upright man, one that feareth God, and escheweth evil?
>
> – Job 1:8

First of all, God had to consider Job of worth and value before he put Job in the showcase. I had to learn while I was in the showcase to wear my high heel shoes well. God will pay you good. Job was paid double for his trouble.

So the LORD blessed the latter end of Job more than his beginning: for he had fourteen thousand sheep, and six thousand camels, and a thousand yoke of oxen, and a thousand she asses.

– Job 42:12

The Lord blessed the latter end of Job more than his beginning. Job's lost and suffering paid off. He was given double for his trouble. In Job 1:3, he had 7000 sheep, 3000 camels, 500 yoke of oxen, 5000 she asses, and a very great household. So, this man was the greatest of all the men of the East. God counted him worthy to suffer. In Job 42:12, God doubled his blessing. Instead of 7,000 sheep, he was blessed to have 14,000 sheep; where he had 3,000 camels, God gave him 6,000 camels; in his beginning, he had 500 yoke of oxen and now he has a 1,000 yoke of oxen; lastly, his 500 she asses doubled to 1,000 she asses. In due time, he had children again, which numbered the same as those he lost in the cyclone of Job 1:19.

And, behold, there came a great wind from the wilderness, and smote the four corners of the house, and it fell upon the young men, and they are dead; and I only am escaped alone to tell thee.

– Job 1:19

You will find in Job 1:18 that the word also came to Job to let him know thy sons and daughters were eating and drinking wine in their eldest brother's house.

Note:
Everything came rapidly of the calamities so as to overwhelm Job all at once if possible.

This is what happens in troubled marriages. A lot of things will start happening rapidly to overwhelm you; to get you to throw in the towel. Trials were coming my way sometimes every week, if not every day. You will become cast down, but not forsaken for you know your Redeemer lives.

All that he had was turned over to Satan and all that was left to him after Satan had finished his work was one servant out of each calamity and his wife who cooperated with the devil in the trial of Job. This is what Satan does. He will cause the closest person to you to come against you.

And a man's foes shall be they of his own household.

– Matthew 10:36

Satan is the author of confusion. God is the author of peace.

In Job's account, Satan was given permission by God to touch all that he had to test Job. God put a limit to Job's testing by Satan.

There hath no temptation taken you but such as is common to man: but God is faithful, who will not suffer you to be tempted above that ye are able; but will with the temptation also make a way to escape, that ye may be able to bear it.

–1 Corinthians 10:13

We see here according to Job's trials, when the great bolt of lightning hit, it would seem to be of God. Today, men consider every storm, all lightning, winds, and other things causing disaster to be the calamity of God, not realizing that the devil is the prince of the power of the air (Ephesians 2:1-3) who is permitted the use of such things in a limited way. It is true that God can also make use of such things, but for men to decide whether it was God or Satan at the permission of God on any particular instance would not be possible.

After Job suffered all lost, he simply arose and refused to blame God as Satan had hoped he would. Now, can God count on you when your marriage is being attacked? Can you stand the test? Wait for the manifestation of God's power to intervene. Sometimes you feel like you have reached your limit and when you feel you can't take or want to take anymore, God always has someone to be there for you if by a call, text, or visit or by the preaching of the word.

Remember the account that I mentioned earlier about this woman's daughter calling to tell on her mother? How she was seeing my husband knowing that he was a married man? Well, after the call, it was a known thing that my husband was seeing this woman especially when the woman told me herself that they had been together for 10 years. I was crushed, but I kept my eyes lifted to the hills from whence cometh my help.

One day, my husband was off from work and I had to go to work that day, but for some reason he carried me to work. I had a knowing in my spirit that after he put me out at work, he did not go home. He went to her house. When I confronted him to let him know I knew by the Spirit that he was at her house after putting me out for work, he could not deny it. That was a sad season in my life. It seems as though my husband could not stop doing the wrong he was doing. I fasted and fasted and I prayed and prayed until one day, I decided I will love the devil out of him.

Now, that was not biblical. The Bible says for us to cast the devil out and it also says in Romans 12:17-19.

Recompense to no man evil for evil. Provide things honest in the sight of all men. If it be possible, as much as lieth in you, live peaceably with all men. Dearly beloved, avenge not yourselves, but rather give place unto wrath: for it is written, Vengeance is mine; I will repay, saith the Lord. Therefore if thine enemy hunger, feed him; if he thirst, give him drink: for in so doing thou shalt heap coals of fire on his head. Be not overcome of evil, but overcome evil with good.

– Romans 12:17-19

I took scriptures like these and applied them to my life to overcome. My marriage vows became real in my Christian life. Therefore, I realized I had duties to perform as a Christian. I also taught myself to abide in the scripture over in 2 Timothy 2:3 to endure hardness as a good soldier of Jesus Christ; 2 Timothy 2:12—if we suffer, we shall also reign with him; 2 Timothy 2:6—the husbandman that laboreth, must be first partakers of the fruits. In these scriptures, I took it literally that if I were going to make full proof of my ministry doing the work as an evangelist as Paul taught, I realized I was going to have to go through some things to be able to help others.

I cannot sit, nor stand, and preach to you about marriage and how to stick with each other like glue except I stood some testing of my marriage vows. Another scripture I took along with me was 2 Timothy 3:12—"Yea, and all that will live godly in Christ Jesus shall suffer persecution."

No it is not God's will that your marriage be unhappy. It is the will of the devil, your adversary, who goes around seeking whomever he may devour especially marriages. God's will is that you love one another and be faithful to one another till death do you part.

CHAPTER TEN

SATAN: THE OPPOSITION

Satan opposes what God ordains and yes, marriage falls into that category.

Marriage is honorable and the bed undefiled, but whoremongers and adulterers, God will judge.

– Hebrews 13:4

Vengeance is mine saith the Lord; I will repay. (Romans 12:19). One Sunday, my husband got himself ready not for church, but to do whatever he would do while the children and I were in church. Very seldom did we miss church. Now, if I had had a baby, then I would stay home up under the rule of that day. After my husband got dressed, he went off because he would rise early and go off in the mornings on the weekends. He came back home and was just pacing the house, so I asked him would he help wash up the kids. He helped a couple of the kids, but unwillingly, and I finished helping them to get ready. My husband stood around until we pulled out in my car and he left behind us.

As I stopped for a light that was close to the church, he had caught up with us and was right behind us. When the light changed, I pulled off going to my left and he went to his right. All of a sudden, I felt led to put the children out for Sunday School. I told them mama needed to go check on something and I'll be right back. That was something I had never done before. I thought to go by that place where I had seen his car parked on that day I was coming from the doctor. On that day, I saw his car parked on the side of the road where some apartment buildings were and he had lied to me and said that he was at a friend's house, but he would never bring friends by our house or invite them so his family could meet them. So, I knew of no such friends he had. I believe I was led to follow him for two reasons.

First of all, I had a suspicion that he had a girlfriend over there because my children would tell me that they had been by the maid's house with their daddy and they would try and describe where she lived. I followed him over to the place where I had seen his car that day and surely it was parked right there where I had seen it before. I was at peace, but I just wanted to see what was going on that day. Secondly, his attitude towards me was so mean-spirited that morning and I was feeling pretty hurt. So, wanting to know why, I followed him. I cannot confess that I was in the right spirit to do what I did. All I can say is I felt led to do it, but to do it peaceably.

After my arrival, I did not know where to go. I got out of my car all dressed for church and I went and knocked at the first apartment door. A big heavy set lady came to the door and I asked her did she know what apartment building the man who was driving that car would be in, but she said no. I thanked her and walked away. As I was walking away though, she got my attention and pointed next door. I thanked her again and walked over to the next door.

A young man answered the door with the door being opened wide without a screen to it. I told him I was looking for my husband and he said he was there. Wait just a minute. Well, I had a boldness on me that day, but I didn't understand where it came from, so as the young man left the door wide open to go upstairs to get my husband or to let him know I was at the door, I just walked up the steps behind him. By the time I reached the top of the stairs, the young man was knocking on a door that was closed and I was standing behind the young man at the door. He called out to my husband to let him know I was there and my husband opened the door while answering the young man.

Now the young man did not say your wife wants to see you; he said that someone wants to see you and I know at my husband's surprise, he never thought it would be me because the last time he saw me, I was going to church with the children. When the door opened, my husband was fully clothed with his gloves on, coat on, and hat; it was a cold day. He was standing in the lady's bedroom with a newspaper in his hand waiting for her to finish getting dressed, so he could carry HER to church. Her daughter was pinning a corsage on her when I asked my husband, "What are you doing in this lady's bedroom?" He replied, "These are friends of mine." I replied, "For a man to be in a woman's bedroom, she has got to mean something to him." He came out of her room by my asking him to, but I never entered the bedroom. I stayed at the door of the room in the hallway. He slowly came out and would not come down the stairs, so I asked him to come downstairs, so I could get out of that lady's house. He finally came down being in a haughty spirit and then I felt like a fool. He pulled off. I pulled off and went on to church and asked for my children. I was too hurt to stay at church. I was hurt double because my husband did not try and comfort me. He talked to me in a bad manner with no remorse. I went home and wallowed in my hurt and tears. He was not home when I got home and that did not make it any better. He came home later with the same mean spirit. Blaming me. I learned later that he would carry that lady to church quite often. My day was very hurtful because my husband had gotten in a bad spirit of lying and not caring.

He would walk in the house from work not speaking for weeks. There were times I deliberately came up front to sit in the living room for him to see me just for him to speak to me. What he would do was nod his head or grunt at me and pass me to go on to his bedroom. I used to hate those days. They were the silent treatment days and solitary months.

One day, I was hurting so from one event to another. Whatever it was, I wanted attention from my husband and the devil got a hold of him where he did not seem to be my husband. He became so possessed by the enemy where he did not count me as his wife. He shut down, pulled away, and did his own thing. During my season of pastoring, I have had some embarrassing moments where I had a daughter in law to invite a co-worker to church service and when the young lady got to church, she discovered that my husband was the man that had been seeing her mother and she would not come back to visit.

All kinds of things of that sort I began to learn and there are just some things I will not reveal. Out of all I had been through, one day the enemy was toying with my emotions. I was being tried on every hand. I decided to leave home and go to my daughter's house for a day or two. While there, he called for me to come back home. Well, I did not return that day for I was trying to get his attention. Surely, I got his attention where he showed up to Bible Study at the church. Normally, he would not come to Bible Study. Although he was a member of the church, he would not come to church or Bible Study, but he knew how to see me and talk to me by coming to Bible Study that particular night.

He asked to see me in the office, but I said no. He got spiritual on me and replied back, "You are my Pastor; now Pastor, can I see you to talk to you?" Now that got me. What could I say, but okay. He entered the office and fell to his knees and asked me to please forgive him; that he was sorry for what he had done to me. My flesh wanted to stand up in me, but I humbled myself and came home that night. I knew if I did what was right, that God would exalt me in due season. That was one assurance that my husband had. He knew I was going to obey the word of the Lord sooner or later. There were many times I would be displeased with my husband, but once I get to church and hear the preaching and teaching of the Gospel, conviction would fall on me and I would return home with a better attitude. Yes, I had to give so much, now I am reaping much.

As I mentioned earlier, he had been seeing one of the ladies and continued to do so because he could not fulfill the promises he would make. Within two weeks, the old man, Ol' Cole, would resurface. As a matter of fact, I don't think he would stop. He could just put on a good face for two weeks.

I gave so much for the power of God was in me. I was a 100-fold Christian and even at that I was not perfect; I was reaching for perfections. When I was carrying one of the last three boys, I was sick and not feeling well some days. I was lonely and miserable. I left the bedroom to enter the kitchen to get something and he was in the kitchen and approached the door way. I had no intentions to hit my husband, but the hurt had built up so intensively where before I knew it, I had hit my husband. Now, what happened, I did not hit him for nothing. He had overlooked me like he did not care about my pain, sickness, nor mistreatment that caused me to retaliate. I admit that I was wrong. I don't care what was happening. I should have never lifted my hand against him. All it did was cause him to leave the house upset at me. I became very remorseful. Although he probably was going to leave anyway, my hitting him did not help matters at all.

That occurred before I began to pastor, but I was saved from my sins, loved Jesus, and I repented for the wrong I had done. That's why you have to stay on your knees in prayer. Married couples, stay prayerful.

I had a sister in Christ whose husband was a bus driver too. She and I would pray together. She would encourage me in the Lord and in my marriage. One day, I decided to let her know that I had found out who my husband's girlfriend was and she informed me that she already knew, but would not say anything to me. She asked if my husband had told me and I said yes; she lives in a certain apartment. She said no, she lives in another apartment building. I said no, it is in this apartment. She replied again, no, it is in another apartment building, so I took thought and came to the conclusion that she and I were talking about two different ladies. I was crushed. I was having a fit over one known relationship for around 10 years and this new relationship that was surfacing was a 12-year relationship!

Later, I called my husband and asked him about the new relationship that I was hearing about. He answered me saying I did not have to worry about it. The lady died the day before. He came home and revealed some things to me. He broke down and told me he was under such attack. He had no idea how to attend the funeral because he knew he would see some people who knew me. He revealed that he had a hard time going to the hospital to see her because some of the church people knew me. He was slipping out to the hospital making visits hoping that no one who knew he was my husband would show up at the time he was there.

He said it had been very hard trying to keep it from me and trying not to be seen at the hospital visiting. Well, I was hurt over the one lady who told me she had been with my husband for 10 years, now I was hurting over this 12-year affair, so I talked with my husband and told him for you to be with a person for 12 years, she must mean something to you. Mind you, she is the person I had went up the stairs and found him waiting for her to finish dressing, so he could carry her to her church.

Also, remember I said earlier in my writing that I would tell you about the beautiful nice suit that my husband wore to his father's funeral? Well, on the day of the girlfriend's funeral, I took that same suit down and told my husband that I would press it for him and he thanked me. I pressed the suit and laid it out for my husband to wear to his woman's funeral. While doing so, he revealed to me that the other 10-year affair woman had picked it out and got it for him to wear for his father's funeral. The Holy Spirit had let me know that there was something peculiar about the suit. My husband also let me know he needed to go by her apartment and see her parents because they hadn't seen him. He also had keys to the apartment that she had given him. I asked him would he leave them because he did not need them anymore and he said yes. I suppose he didn't; I really don't know. He wanted to go to the funeral. He felt obligated to be there, so I did not object to him going. I pressed his suit to look good. He left to go to her house and greet her parents for they knew him; he had carried her to see them on certain occasions out of town. I got myself and my daughter ready to go by the church just to look on this woman and I did. She was lying in the church before the funeral and I went in with Jesus in my heart and came out with Jesus in my heart. I only looked on her, but my daughter was young and humorous and she said, "Oh look mama, she was pretty." Her words crushed my spirit. I was already wondering what she had that I didn't have. For my daughter to admire her beauty was hurtful, but I left out peaceful and went on home finding my husband soon coming home. He said he went by to see the body at the church and her parents at her house and I asked him did he leave her key at her house. He said yes. After seeing her parents, he did not bother to go to the funeral. It was his choice. I was kind and affectionate to him because he had lost someone who was a part of him for 12 years. Not that I was glad of the relationship nor the death.

My husband explained that so many times he wanted to end relationships, but when he would not call or drop by, the women would call him. He revealed to me that he would tell his women about my revival meetings at various churches trying to get them saved. I understand from him that there were times they would come to my services. Now, these were just two, but there were others. Many others that I am also aware of. After then, I asked him to tell me all about him and his relationships out of the two and he did. He disclosed some things that I will not repeat, but I will never do that again. It is too hurtful and I had to promise him that I would not get angry or bring it up to him. After he revealed some things, it was very hurtful, but I could not say a word or react to what I had heard.

Ladies, it is not good for you. You don't really want to know what went on. You may think you do; then, you learn we all are not alike. See, one thing I learned is that my husband could not let a day go by without making contact and he is married with 7 children with me and his oldest son makes 8 children besides the miscarriage I had.

Now, my life had taken on another leaf. The things that were told to me, crushed me every day and night. For one whole year, the devil made sure he rehearsed those two affairs to me. I would wake up with it on my mind. Driving myself to work five days a week, I would play the song "He Will Take My Gloom" and cry all the way to work and back. While on the job, the devil would rehearse one relationship all morning, then by noon time until quitting time, he would rehearse the second relationship. After one year of my finding out, I told God I couldn't take it. It's about to kill me and I dropped that big ball of pressure and hurt and gave all of it to Jesus and he delivered me as soon as I dropped it and gave it up. I had to let self die—the flesh man had to get over it.

CHAPTER ELEVEN

SECRETS TO SURVIVING YOUR MARRIAGE

As I journeyed on, my husband began to get better towards me, but not 100%. Other problems were floating, but I did not feel like I was drowning. I asked the Lord to take the hurt out of the hurt and he did. Things would occur. I would feel it, but it wouldn't hurt me. God did a marvelous work in me. I had to allow Him to do it. It was not against my will. I willed to be healed, to recover, and I kept myself busy, lifted, humble, and loving.

While I was working, my husband began to get home before me and he started cooking dinner and having it ready for me; he started being more concerned, and what I did, I kept my praise hot. I kept working for the Lord. I began to feel my Helper in a greater way. I stopped crying all the time, I stopped going to bed at night with my heart heavy, and my face tight. I started resting in Jesus. You won't lose by being humble. The humble child tastes the grace. I survived from the life support of the word of God. It kept me, freed me, comforted me, and delivered me. I am free, free indeed. I stood my test and yet standing, but it was not easy.

Here is what I had to do:

1. I made a decision to love.
   Love starts with a decision

2. I made a decision to recover.
   Recovery starts with a decision.

3. I allowed God to take the hurt out of the hurt.

4. I had to get over my coming home to find the telephone cord still dangling.

#5. I did not know my marriage vows well, but I knew God's word. I practiced His word in my life situation.

If you are to survive your marriage, you must do them too; you must start with these tips to help you make the decision to fight for your marriage.

How to Survive Your Marriage

To survive your marriage, you are to rely on God's principles and His biblical counsel, not those of the world. The principles I am sharing with you are from the word of God. I lived and applied them to my life situation and witnessed the true manifestation of God's power. I tried these principles and they worked for me.

Principles

- God promises if you delight in him, commit your ways to him, trust him completely, rest in him and wait patiently, he will give you the desires of your heart. **(Psalm 37:4-5)**
- Don't withhold sex from your husband **(1 Corinthians 7:4-5)**
- You may be every woman, a bag of chips, and all of that, but stop being a fighting chicken and let the little girl come out of you.
- Good marriages are made by faith, love, determination, and hard work.
- God instituted marriage before any other law.
- Know your spouse. Wives know your husbands and husbands know your wives.
- God gave Adam a suitable helpmeet.
- My husband loved me for my kindness.

- For the fruit of the spirit, he saw and witnessed in me.
- Do not leave the Word of God out of your marriage.
- Commit your marriage to God.
- God will reward your prayers. **(Hebrews 10:35-36)**
- You cannot be puffed up, angry at God, and expect Him to move for you.
- Forgive. (**Ephesians 4:32)**

In the midst of these, be kind and compassionate to each other, forgiving each other, just as in Christ, God forgave you. Be kind to each other, tenderhearted, forgiving just as God, through Christ, has forgiven you. Remember, God not only forgave us, but gave us himself.

- Be confident and patient.
- Give yourself to the marriage.
- Don't fail to give yourself away.
- Tie a knot at the end of the rope and hold on.
- Don't give up.
- Acknowledge your wrong doing.
- Grow and stay connected.
- Be a good helpmeet.
- When you're having marriage problems, don't throw in the towel.
- Hold on to the strings of it.
- Learn how to iron the wrinkles out.
- Don't go buy another man or woman, fix this one.
- Don't give place to the devil.
- Always remember Satan is the author of confusion.
- The keyword is *love*; love Jesus above all.

- Another key word is *submit*; submit to authority of Christ Jesus and the authority of your husband.
- Don't be in despair, loss of hope, or hopelessness.
- God will resurrect your marriage.
- There's nothing God can't do.
- Be willing to pay the price.
- Women pray until you hear God speaking back to you saying I see and I know.
- Keep a prayer on your lips and a care in your heart.
- Learn to forgive and rebuild your marriage.
- In every battle, you will need faith as your shield to stop the fiery darts and arrows aimed at you by Satan.
- Take the sword of the spirit, which is the word of God, and whip the Devil.
- Draw a line in your spirit declaring "Devil you won't have my marriage!"
- Declare war on the enemy of your soul, the adversary the devil, and don't let him defeat you by not giving up; continue to speak positively over your marriage.
- No matter what your eyes may see and your ears may hear, keep speaking; this too will pass.
- Yes, know by a sure word of prophecy that this too will pass. Like a woman who is pregnant, sooner or later, when the time is right, the fruit from her womb will fall and come forth. In due time, surely it will not tarry at the appointed time.

I survived 55 years of marriage by taking God's Word as my life support.

I took God's words for just what they said; it is no longer an eye for an eye nor a tooth for a tooth. I had to accept the Word of the Lord where he says in Romans 12:17.

Recompense to no man evil for evil. Provide things honest in the sight of all men. If it be possible, as much as lieth in you, live peaceably with all men. Dearly beloved, avenge not yourselves, but rather give place unto wrath: for it is written, Vengeance is mine; I will repay, saith the Lord. Therefore if thine enemy hunger, feed him; if he thirst, give him drink: for in so doing thou shalt heap coals of fire on his head. Be not overcome of evil, but overcome evil with good.

– Romans 12:17

I lived and breathed those scriptures and that is how I endured my affliction and became a hard soldier. Knowing, according to Psalm 34:15-18,

The eyes of the LORD are upon the righteous, and his ears are open unto their cry. The face of the LORD is against them that do evil, to cut off the remembrance of them from the earth. The righteous cry, and the LORD heareth, and delivereth them out of all their troubles. The LORD is nigh unto them that are of a broken heart; and saveth such as be of a contrite spirit.

–Psalm 34:15-18,

I would allow him to strengthen me. When I felt that the mistreatment from my husband was overwhelming, Psalm 34:19 would come up in my spirit.

Many are the afflictions of the righteous, but the Lord delivereth him out of them all.

–Psalm 34:19

When trouble kept on rising and I thought I was about to faint, I remembered Isaiah 40:28-31.

Hast thou not known? hast thou not heard, that the everlasting God, the LORD, the Creator of the ends of the earth, fainteth not, neither is weary? there is no searching of his understanding. He giveth power to the faint; and to them that have no might he increaseth strength. Even the youths shall faint and be weary, and the young men shall utterly fall: But they that wait upon the LORD shall renew their strength; they shall mount up with wings as eagles; they shall run, and not be weary; and they shall walk, and not faint.

–Isaiah 40:28-31

My strength would be renewed from the power of the word. I would find myself being willing to wait upon the Lord patiently and being of good courage; being of good cheer and staying in church and praying with the people of God. By doing so, I would have eventually come to the conclusion that my husband was not my enemy. The devil was using him as the enemy.

By realizing and having an understanding that the power was within me, I had to give more. Much more I had to deal with. I was a 100-fold Christian and he was none. Then, I had to deal with my 100-fold Christian dedication and his 30 to 60-fold dedication. You can do it, just as I did, because like me, you have the enablement, your assistant, the Holy Ghost.

But he that knew not, and did commit things worthy of stripes, shall be beaten with few stripes. For unto whomsoever much is given, of him shall be much required: and to whom men have committed much, of him they will ask the more.

–Luke 12:48

Ye are of God, little children, and have overcome them: because greater is he that is in you, than he that is in the world.

–1 John 4:4

The Spirit of God was greater in me than the devil who was using my husband.

Therefore, I allowed myself to love and take more, forgive more, love more, humble myself more, be kindhearted more, endure longsuffering more, be peaceful more, be faithful more, be joyous more, and be gentle more. I had to let goodness, meekness, and temperance prevail.

I made a decision that I was not going to violate my sacred vows. I was tempted by the devil, but I ate from the Lord's table daily.

There hath no temptation taken you but such as is common to man: but God is faithful, who will not suffer you to be tempted above that ye are able; but will with the temptation also make a way to escape, that ye may be able to bear it.

–1 Corinthians 10:13

I remember there was a time in my life where the devil, the old tempter, tried to get me to bow to his temptations, but with the Holy Spirit being inside me and my yielding to him, I was able to yield myself unto righteousness.

Know ye not, that to whom ye yield yourselves servants to obey, his servants ye are to whom ye obey; whether of sin unto death, or of obedience unto righteousness?

– Romans 6:16

It is not sin to be tempted; the sin is in yielding. I willed to not bend or bow. I kept focus and kept my eyes to the hills from whence cometh my help. Certain places I did not go and certain things I did not do. Through reconciliation, the Lord gave me the Ministry of Reconciliation. I had to keep in remembrance 2 Corinthians 5:17-20.

Therefore if any man be in Christ, he is a new creature: old things are passed away; behold, all things are become new. And all things are of God, who hath reconciled us to himself by Jesus Christ, and hath given to us the ministry of reconciliation; To wit, that God was in Christ, reconciling the world unto himself, not imputing their trespasses unto them; and hath committed unto us the word of reconciliation. Now then we are ambassadors for Christ, as though God did beseech you by us: we pray you in Christ's stead, be ye reconciled to God.

–2 Corinthians 5:17-20

I had to come to grips with the fact that if I have a calling on my life to win souls for the Kingdom, I had to know that God would have me to start at home first among my own household. That is why I learned how to love and care for my husband who was first in my life before going into the world. Charity begins in the home and then it spreads abroad.

I kept in mind that I could not go to the world and preach Jesus and His love when I could not love my own husband and render reconciliation unto him. I always came back to my husband when we had our differences to make sure we were friendly again (Reconciliation). I had to grow into it. Every aspect of my life, I had to grow into another level of faith and another dimension of His glory.

It took a death of my flesh. I had to die daily to the things of the flesh. I had to kill out the fight that was within me. One reason why I hurt and cried so much is because I did not want to put down my sword; my weapon of self-defense. I had to cross-over from the fleshly field to the kingdom of light.

Jesus said, ‘If any man come after me, let him take up his cross and follow me; let him deny himself.’ (Matthew 16:24). Once you come to grips that his yoke is easy and burden is light, then you can rest in the Lord and let his will be done. The will of the Father, not mine, be done.

CHAPTER TWELVE

WILLING TO HOLD OUT

I suffered much for a long time for years. Remember, my marriage started off wrong with no full commitment to the marriage from my husband. I beg of you not to start off that way for it is too hard of a task. It takes a lot of selling out to Christ, which is a good thing. However, it takes a willingness and a denied life to conquer the enemy of your marriage—the old devil.

If ye be willing and obedient, ye shall eat the good of the land:
–Isaiah 1:19

I applied this scripture to my married life also. If I be willing to hold out and see God work this thing out for my good, then I shall eat the good things of the land concerning my marriage. Having the Lord in my life was worth it.

Now unto him that is able to do exceeding abundantly above all that we ask or think, according to the power that worketh in us.
– Ephesians 3:20

God has done for me to an extent, which I cannot express. His amazing and unlimited power has shifted me to a dimension of Grace with His favor, which is so amazing. In everything, I have suffered, He has blessed me for it. You cannot beat God in giving. The more you give, the more He gives to you. Don't be afraid to endure hardness as a good soldier of Jesus Christ. It was worth having the Lord in my life. My life has turned for the good.

My husband's spirit has turned towards God and now he can please me the rest of his life.

Yes, serving the Lord will pay off after a while. There are many blessings that await you when you finish your course. Maybe your course is not from your marriage, which is good; however, whatever course you may have to take, apply the word of God to every class. Your answer will be in His word. You don't have to spend money going to a psychologist. They are for the mentally ill and you are only taking a test and your answer book is Jesus and His scriptures. He will give you every answer you need. He will give you answers from a song, Bible verse, sermon, through praise and worship, from a preacher, pastor, evangelist, teacher, prophet, apostle, or whomever He chooses. You just have to stay open; keep your eyes, ears, and heart open to hear God and not what you want to hear, but what He is saying directly to you. Let your spirit witness what God is saying. Keep yielding to His word. You are only going through in order to come out of all your afflictions.

As Job suffered boils on his body, lost all his seven children, had a wife speaking as a foolish woman, his possessions and his health taken away, it seemed there was trouble on every side for Job, but God was ever-present. Job suffered much disaster. His wife told him to curse God and die (Job 2:9). Job replied, 'What? Shall we receive good at the hand of God and shall we not receive evil? (Job 2:10). According to the scripture, Job did not curse God, but cursed his day, which was still wrong. He had what we call an overpowering day, but the Lord did not leave Job; he yet blessed Job. As God blessed Job, God blessed me.

I had a four-bedroom all over brick house with a large yard for my children to play. I had it decorated inside very nicely. Some would come and ask did I get an interior decorator to design the house. My reply was no, I decorated my house, which I did. My husband, after putting me through so much for so many years, (you better know there was so much more that went on that I won't reveal) is paying me well now. One thing I can say is Satan may touch all you have, but he can't touch you. As much as he tried, he could never touch me. I never lost my praise. Women, keep your praise hot and a prayer on your lips through the tribulations of your marriage. God will see you through.

[12] And the LORD said unto Satan, Behold, all that he hath is in thy power; only upon himself put not forth thine hand. So Satan went forth from the presence of the LORD.

–Job 1:12

The devil touched my marriage, but he could not lay a hand on me. Someone even tried to make me believe that someone had worked witchcraft on me, but I did not believe or accept it. I kept the door closed to witchcraft. You have to have an open door for witchcraft to work on you. Remember that.

My husband became remorseful, repented to me, and began to do things to please me. Not that I requested those things, but that was his way to show me love and not just speak love, but to show me in his deeds. Everything that is within his power, he tries to give it to me now.

The first thing he wanted me to have was a new house. He purchased me a brand new home in a gated community where I wanted to live. He did not have the faith as I did, but he was willing to follow the Holy Spirit in my life. We came looking for a home together in this subdivision. We had the choice to choose from two houses. One was down the street; very pretty, but somewhat small. The other house was on the corner of the 3rd Street in the subdivision and it was large. Well, my husband was afraid to look inside of that house for he thought it was too much of a house inside plus the price was expensive. He chose a smaller house down the street because he felt like that was all we needed because all the children were gone and grown. I liked the larger home better and because it was up front in the subdivision.

I remember prophesying myself in that gated community right in the area the house was sitting. I chose the house where I prophesied I would live one day and it came to pass! I told God this is the house I want and I was given one month to have everything finished to move in. The Lord blessed me to get my down payment money and my own mortgage broker and we were ready in one month. I have been in that house for 16 years. My husband wanted to put me in another home and he did with the help of the Lord. I witnessed the scripture that says he that will come shall come and will not tarry (Hebrews 10:37). God was in it and He had blessings for me to receive now and not over on the other side. He intended for me to enjoy my blessings in the land of the living. I was blessed to furnish my house—every room with some of the nicest quality pieces of designer furniture. I love my Lord. What He has promised, He will perform. The Lord put in my husband's heart to bless me and treat me as a queen. When I was working, the day came when I would arrive home from work and my dinner would be cooked and served to me. My clothes would be washed and folded and my slippers ready for me to put on. God tamed that lion in my husband and caused him to entreat me as a loving wife. One young lady would say, "God tamed that lion in him because he was so mean where not one of us liked him." She was speaking of her sisters and cousins and some friends who would come to the church revivals and house services and she made known to me that none of them liked him because he was so mean to me. She would say, "We wanted to jump on him and beat him." Yet, they love him today. They see the transformation that has been done in his life and they are friendly; he is like their godfather.

My husband is 8-years older than I am and he wanted me to have everything I wanted before he leaves here. A friend wanted me to take over her Mercedes-Benz and my husband wanted me to have it because he knew I wanted one, so he sacrificed and paid for that Mercedes. I am enjoying my car and it is paid off now. Before the Mercedes-Benz, I wanted a 300 Chrysler. It was specially designed in a very beautiful midnight blue color with a cloth top; very admirable and I got it with my husband purchasing it for me; it is paid off too.

As I write now, my husband is cooking breakfast for me. He cooks breakfast all the time for me. He will fix my lunch also and he cooks dinner a lot for me. He not only cooks for me, he serves me my food, pours up my juices, water, and coffee, and removes my plate raking my food from it and he washes it. I am not lazy and my husband knows it, but he does these things because he says he wants to do it and loves doing it and I deserve it.

I know my duties as a wife. It is his choice to do these things for me. He loves for me to come home and find dishes washed, the kitchen mopped, and the house freshened up. When I go off, it gives him pleasure for me to come home with the house smelling good, food cooked, and the clothes washed and folded. He loves keeping the yards clean. He asks that I don't take the yards from him by calling in a yard care service. He wants to do his own yard.

He is so committed to the things of the house. He doesn’t like for me to carry my car to be washed; he likes washing my car himself. Now, he loves me to praise him for what he does and I do. I am very thankful for all that he does and it gives me more time for ministry.

One thing is he is not a jelly back man. He is his own man. He doesn't like for me to ask him to do things. He likes to do what he wants to do and surprise me with it. Therefore, he is always doing things that he feels I will appreciate. Some things I hate to reveal because you may feel that I'm just a no-good wife, but not so. He is an early riser, so he rises early and does things early. Early in the morning, he makes the coffee; early in the morning, he makes the bed, and that is what he likes to do. By the time I get up, his work is almost finished. He still works part-time. He is a phenomenal man; a good and hard-working man; a man who has always provided for his family.

I have his attention now. God has His attention and we praise God for what has happened in his life. I asked my husband what happened to make him change. He replied, “You.” He then began to explain what he meant. He said, “How you put up with my foolishness. I would do things to make you mad, but you would not stay mad long and I saw what a good wife I had to put up with that. Most of all, God saved me. You were a great inspiration to me—how you lived your life.”

Yes, my worship was for real. That's how I survived 55 years of marriage with my adulterous husband. I learned to turn my pain into praise! I am in my triumphant chariot on this side of Heaven. I kept His word in remembrance. I was born to win! I was the expressed image of God. I knew the Lord as my shepherd and I shall not want. He is grand and amazing. I am justified by faith. I belong to the King of Kings. Jesus is my hero. I didn't have to look back down to the devil. I knew that the blood of Jesus took care of everything.

If you suffer with him, you shall reign with him. ‘Thy word have I hid in my heart that I might not sin against thee’ (Psalm 119:11). Let me shut it down! God will reward you! I am in my rewarding stage. Genesis 21:6, Sarah said, God hath made me to laugh, so that all that hear will laugh with me. Women, I beseech you to let go of your faith and praise! God will cause you to laugh again.

And the LORD visited Sarah as he had said, and the LORD did unto Sarah as he had spoken. For Sarah conceived, and bare Abraham a son in his old age, at the set time of which God had spoken to him.

– Genesis 21:1-2

God renewed Sarah's youth, so that she could bear a child and nurse him (vv. 1-2.). With every episode I encountered, God renewed me where I received strength from above. By receiving strength from above, my baby leaped and caused joy to fill my soul and I began to prophesy and declare supernatural happenings for my marriage. I began to declare that my husband was saved and I wouldn't take it back no matter what was going on and how he was behaving. I declared deliverance for my marriage. I began to be happy because my trust was in God.

I will bless the LORD at all times: his praise shall continually be in my mouth. My soul shall make her boast in the LORD: the humble shall hear thereof, and be glad. O magnify the LORD with me, and let us exalt his name together.

–Psalm 34:1-3

I would praise and declare the blessings of the Lord! God's power performed and brought my heart's desire to pass. Don't give up. Abraham was 100 years old when the birth of Isaac was released. You have to make a marriage just as you have to make a baby. It is time consuming, but you have to work on it. Work it out by the word of the Lord.

To get to the glory of the marriage, suffering is in the globe. The journey isn't free; the dream is.

It costs to be a good woman willing to pay the price. Continue to be a well-kept woman by the power of God whose rank is royalty. Misery has been your company, but laughter is on the way. Start laughing now. I declare a blessing of laughter and not failure. He is ready to give you reconciliation. Look to God for your miracle. See God turning your marriage into a good relationship. Get ready to receive your past due blessing.

God is ready. Do you hear what I am saying? God is ready to give more than you can ask or think! I never thought my husband would serve me as he does. I do not have to cook, clean, or wash clothes. He doesn't demand anything from me, but he used to. I used to have to get up at 4:00 in the morning and fix breakfast. I've gotten slapped on the head because for Friday evening dinner, there was nothing except Pot Pie served, but that was all that we had left from grocery that week. However, it was because I went to church that night to a revival service that the devil used my husband to strike me across my head because he had not had a full meal and I was not home. I was in church.

Back in the day, money was limited and there was not much left for Friday. At least I cooked what I had. Today, I control the money and walk in my abundance. I want you to know there's a hidden blessing in your storm. There's nothing my God can't do. Getting a divorce because you are having problems is not the answer. If you don't allow God to fix it, you only carry these problems over into the other marriage. Most times, your issues are you. Get yourself out of the equation.

God allowed my husband to drive the nails killing my ego and pride. The flesh has to be crucified. Romans 8:13 says ‘ for if you live after the flesh, ye shall die; but if ye through the spirit do mortify the deeds of the body, ye shall live.’ This is one of my favorite scriptures that kept me yielded to the Holy Spirit that God may be glorified in my life.

My husband was able to see a yielded vessel; a vessel of honor and not dishonor. I understand the spirit of cheating and how the devil will tempt an individual who has been wounded and hurt by his or her spouse. I remember when my heart would become saddened and lonely, I would get me a scripture and quote it or sing me a song of deliverance such as Psalm 34:1. 'I will bless the Lord at all times; his praise shall continually be in my mouth.'

I would realize even in my time of temptation, my soul shall make her boast in the Lord. I would not give place to the devil. He would be talking and talking good stuff like showing me where to go and who would be glad to see me, but I had to deny myself and you have to deny yourself—the flesh man—and tell it no! Remind yourself that there is no one who is able to separate you from the Lord. Our perfect example is Jesus.

And when the tempter came to him, he said, If thou be the Son of God, command that these stones be made bread. But he answered and said, It is written, Man shall not live by bread alone, but by every word that proceedeth out of the mouth of God.

– Matthew 4:3

After Jesus' anointing was when temptation came from the devil. Jesus quoted the word from the scripture to him. He had to fight the devil with the word of the Lord. Jesus was tempted of the devil, so surely you and I will be tempted also.

At your most vulnerable time is when the tempter will come. He will do sneak attacks when you are feeling helpless, weak, powerless, or especially when your husband isn't paying any attention to you. Especially when you feel you need special care and support from your husband and you don't feel protected, but neglected and old. All of these are physical and emotional wounds, hurt, and mental attacks.

It is very hurtful when you become older and you know your husband is attracted to younger women because you were very young when you met him. Yet, you are younger than him, but he is still yet amused over young women. That is when you have to encourage yourself in the Lord and quote Psalm 139:14.

I will praise thee; for I am fearfully and wonderfully made; marvelous are thy works; and that my soul knoweth right well.

– Psalm 139:14

You must realize that you are unique, set apart, marvelous, admirable, excellent, very good, and splendid. You are God's handiwork.

He is my strength, teacher, goodness, fortress, high tower, deliverer, shield, trust, conqueror, salvation, buckler, shield, table, water, pavilion, hiding place, my noonday, and my tomorrow. I had to remember the scripture that said in 1 Corinthians 6:19-20,

What? know ye not that your body is the temple of the Holy Ghost which is in you, which ye have of God, and ye are not your own? For ye are bought with a price: therefore glorify God in your body, and in your spirit, which are God's.

–1 Corinthians 6:19-20

Most of all, you never want to displease the Lord nor your mate. You know it will be hurtful to them. If there is one who has committed adultery on his wife, here is some advice for you to use to get your credibility back and to prove to her that you love her and want her forgiveness and trust back.

Listen, your wife is hurting beyond measure now and it will take some time and effort for her to be healed. Her wound is open and it is going to take much love to be poured on that open wound that it may heal. She's going through a lot of frustration, disappointment, betrayal with the devil rehearsing what has happened to her all the day long. The best thing you can do for her is to assure her that you are sorrowful for what you allowed to happen; and that you are through with that relationship; and you want a life with her; and for her to forgive you; and you will prove to her that you love her; and never intend to hurt her again.

Be there for her. Minister to her every need. If it is intimacy, conversation, or whatever she needs, minister that particular thing to her with much prayer and praise and see God work. Declare and decree over your marriage. Let the devil know, you will not have my marriage. Be careful. Don't let the devil cause you to throw your 1 year, 5 years, or 10 years of marriage away. Learn to work through the marriage. Value your marriage vows. You must remember you took an oath before God and others witnessing that you would love, cherish, and care for one another till death do you part. You took those vows before a Holy God.

Women stay a holy woman for a holy woman outclasses them all. It may have been a very attractive woman that came between you and your husband, but you outclassed her for the mere reason you are a pure set aside woman. Therefore, don't become one of them. Don't allow the enemy of your marriage, the devil, to entice you to cheat back on your husband; it is not worth it.

The secret of winning your husband over on your side is through your pure and chaste humble behaviors. I am a living witness that where the power is, the supernatural power of God outweighs all fleshly manipulative power.

The safest way and God's way is to stay in prayer with counsel from God's word and if there be any seasoned Mothers of Zion in your church setting, get encouragement from them.

Remember it is through obedience to God's word with submitting to the headship of your husband, saved or unsaved as long as it doesn't cause you to commit sinful acts, that you win your husband over to your side. Even if you are right, you have to submit to his authority and by doing so, many times, God will step in and cause him to accept the truth concerning the matter from you. It's a God thing; not a fleshly thing. Isaiah 1:19, 'if you be willing and obedient you shall eat the good of the land.'

The will of God is that you be friendly again. **RECONCILED.** You've been bought with a price; the precious blood of Jesus. Shut your mouth and let grace work for you for God uses storms to bless you, not just good things. Let your delight be in the Lord and He will give you the desires of your heart. When it is raining or snowing in your marriage, you can't stop. Delight!

Don't let the devil have your property—your husband. He is yours. You have the deed and title. Don't let the devil make you think your husband is not yours. Learn to love like God intended. Live as ever expecting the return of the Lord neither give place to the devil (Ephesians 4:27). Don't pull away from your spouse and leave him or her to have to wrestle with demonic sexual forces.

CHAPTER THIRTEEN
MARRIAGE NUGGETS

I am persuaded that most married people don't know what marriage is. Marriage is a life committed to each other and not just sex and money. Mother wants to help you. I can't go to heaven full. I must empty out. These marriage nuggets will help you make sense of the turmoil happening in your marriage and prepare you to combat them with the word of God.

MARRIAGE NUGGET #1
Present Your Body

I beseech you therefore, brethren, by the mercies of God, that ye present your bodies a living sacrifice, holy, acceptable unto God, which is your reasonable service.

–Romans 12:1

Listen:

Some of you men who are married, are married, but shacking. What are you saying Mother? What does it mean to be married but shacking? It's like this.

You have a wife at home and another woman who you shack with. Well, what is shacking? Shacking is to move in or live with someone as a lover and live in sin, shacking up for 5 to 10 years or more.

To the Married:

You spontaneously spend the night with the lover and lie making excuses of having to work that night or the truck broke down and you won't make it home tonight.

Married men, I admonish you, go home to your wife. If you say she is dull and use that as a reason to stay out, change. You are the head. You cause her to light up. Put a smile on her face. Dine her and romance her and stop treating her as a slave girl to bear your children and take care of them; cook your food and wash your clothes and keep the house clean plus do 8 hours on another man's job. After all this, all you can see is dullness? No, what you are seeing is tiredness and most times, she's unloved. Just because a woman has babies does not all the time mean she is loved. In fact, in many instances, she's been had and she's tired.

The woman you cohabit and sleep with, but not married to, is simply your sex partner. Most times, she is the one who gets the attention because you want to make sure you don't leave anything undone, so another 'shacker' won't be dropping into her bed. You make sure you are looking in her face and eyes to say, "Please don't have another lover." In the meantime, what about your wife? She knows when there is another person because you can't give your all to her. Guilt is present; you become uneasy with your spouse. Words become shorter; attention span shorter; affection lesser and then coldness of the heart sets in.

I admonish you to turn back to your first love and do your first work over. Start a new beginning in your marriage. First, make a decision of loving her as your wife as Christ loved the church and gave himself for the church. Give yourself to your wife not holding back any of yourself for anyone else. Turn your back on all other interests and turn your face and affection toward your wife. Become intimate (into me you see) with her giving all and holding back none.

MARRIAGE NUGGET #2

A Double-Minded Man Is Unstable in All His Ways

To be double-minded is to have double ways, double standards, and double actions. You have a marriage certificate for one woman, but you serve multiple. You own one house, but you lodge at several houses. Your income tax return says married, but you take care of more than your spouse.

Doublemindedness is not appropriate in God's standard. Your eye is to be single, not full of lust. Don't let the devil in! If so, he will take charge of your marriage and shift it completely opposite of the will of God. I have seen him take husbands and transform them into another creature where the wife would wonder where her husband is. Have you allowed this in your marriage? Have you allowed your wife to wonder where is the man she married? If so, please, by the mercies of God, return back to your first love.

MARRIAGE NUGGET #3

Old School Talk to New School Women

What is old-school talk? It is right down to earth talk meaning it is not hard to understand. It is right to the point, so let's get to the point.

Women your husband does not want to smell gravy and baby milk on you all the time; for instance, if he is the type to make house visits to other women's homes, I guarantee you, he will be smelling a fragrance that says draw me nearer or closer to you; I want to be where you are; Can you stay all night; I wish I could.

You must learn how to awake from sleep and stay awake. If he is tipping, cause him to always want to come back to your lap and bosom. Don't let no other woman rub your husband's head better than you and stroke his spine and back better than you. Let it remain that he's yours.

Listen, little girls (my pet name for you) maybe money was little when you got engaged and married. Perhaps, there was not a wedding band purchased for your husband and I understand that for I have been there, but my advice to you now is to go and buy him a ring signifying he is taken. He's on the job and everywhere he needs to be, but there's no identification of him being a married man. The ring could stop some advances.

I love you ladies with the love of the Lord. I want to see you prosper in your marriages and be happy, which is why I am having this old-school talk with you. Women, you must learn to stop being selfish. It is not all about you now. You are not just losing weight because you want to. Now, you are losing weight also because he wants you to. The scripture says for you to please your husband and that means in everything, not just in the bedroom, but to give him his heart's desire. If he likes you with the black hair, then please him with black hair. If he likes it long, then stop cutting it; put the scissors down. Now, when you were alone, all by yourself and did not have a husband, then you did as you pleased, but not now. For you have been joined with your husband to become one flesh. That is why the scripture says you are to please your husband and the husband is to please his wife, so you can both be on the same accord. It's nothing wrong with coming into agreement and seeing like your husband sees and having your husband to see like you see. This is one of the major problems in marriages. Couples never actually partner and never come into the oneness of each other to fulfill the call of marriage.

God called the women to be subject to their own husbands in everything (Ephesians 5:24) that is lawful and right, but not in things criminal and wrong. If the husband is sinful and demands his wife to leave off the things that save the soul, she is not under obligation to him. Her God and soul must come first. Matthew 22:37, love God more than all else to be saved. Luke 14:26-27, obedience to the husband in all things is based upon him loving his wife, as Christ does the church. Ephesians 5:25, 28, and 33. Read the book and get an understanding. God is going to get you men for not doing a husband's duty and women you must line up accordingly. Repent and turn your marriages to God.

MARRIAGE NUGGET #4
Pastors Do Not Abandon Your Wives

To you pastors who have abandoned your wives, turn back to her. You once wanted a wife, some of you, but now you just want a First Lady who has no rights to play the role as your wife. She has no benefits, but the role as First Lady to be put on exhibit for Sunday and anniversaries. After that, she is not needed anymore. As far as you are concerned, she is just your make-believe wife; she makes you look good for the organization, but not for the Kingdom because the Kingdom of God does not operate on those principles.

A wife is a married woman considered in relation to her spouse, her partner for life, to love and hold till death do you part. God requires that you love her as Christ loved the church and gave himself for it. You can help your wife to be all that she needs to be by being there for her, conversing with her, and having her as your wife, and not a convenient object called the First Lady who is used to cover you and be there for you when you need to look good in the congregation at the conferences. After then, she is considered by you to be no lady unless she is the First Lady or the pastor’s wife. Pastors, get it together. It is holiness or hell and everyone is going to give an account of the deeds done in our body. God forbid that you play with the sanctity of marriage.

MARRIAGE NUGGET #5
He Sleeps By Me/
God Designed Marriage to Include Sex

Marriage is not to be void of sex. God designed sex to be had in the context of marriage. Today, too many engage in this act ordained for marriage prior to marriage creating all sorts of demonic soul ties and opening themselves up to Satan's sex demons. To you married couples, you have God's permission to engage and become one with each other, yet you refuse. You, instead, seek other means of sexual gratification. Why aren't you sleeping with your wife man of God?

And the LORD God caused a deep sleep to fall upon Adam, and he slept: and he took one of his ribs, and closed up the flesh instead thereof; And the rib, which the LORD God had taken from man, made he a woman, and brought her unto the man. And Adam said, This is now bone of my bones, and flesh of my flesh: she shall be called Woman, because she was taken out of Man. Therefore shall a man leave his father and his mother, and shall cleave unto his wife: and they shall be one flesh. And they were both naked, the man and his wife, and were not ashamed.

– Genesis 2:21-25

They were not ashamed for one reason. She was his rib. She came out from him. She was made from him and given his name woman meaning she-man (womb man). She was taken out of man's side, some say to be equal with him while others say from under his arm to be protected by him, and still, others say from near his heart to be loved by him. One thing is for sure and that is she was not taken out of man's head to be lorded over by him, nor from his feet to be trampled on by him.

I believe the scripture where it states in Genesis 2:21 that the Lord God caused a deep sleep to fall upon Adam and he slept; and he took one of his ribs and closed up the flesh instead thereof v.22 and the rib, which the Lord God had taken from man, made he a woman and brought her unto the man.

And from v. 23, the marriage took place after God formed and shaped Eve. He brought Eve unto Adam, gave her to Adam, and Adam accepted her as his wife and profoundly proclaimed that this is now bone of my bone and flesh of my flesh.

She is considered the weaker vessel to the degree she did not come from the dust of the ground, but Adam did. And she came out from Adam. God, according to Genesis 2:7, molded or squeezed and shaped Adam from the dust of the ground that was his body, but the soul and spirit, the inner man were created. Man is to stand side, dwell with, understand, and see her as a vessel to honor, respect, and care for her as the weaker vessel. That does not mean she is less valuable or she does not have equal access to grace.

1 Peter 3:7 says,

[7]Likewise, ye husbands, dwell with them according to knowledge, giving honour unto the wife, as unto the weaker vessel, and as being heirs together of the grace of life; that your prayers be not hindered.

This is rather a basis for a husband to treat his wife with understanding tenderness and patience. So, a word to all you impatient, hard talking, selfish men, who don't sleep with your wife because of different reasons. Well, listen real good. This is Mother speaking.

God has put you as the ruling factor in her life called to be her head. (Ephesians 5: 22-23) You have her submit to you when you get your sex fulfillment and then you exit the room. Did not Peter tell you, you had to be patient with her? She needs your attention after the thrill because a lot of times you are the only one who was fulfilled. Peter told you according to his writing in 1 Peter 3:7 that she is more frail and delicate (weaker) than you. You must treat her with love. A lot of times, you come in like a freight train and mess up everything by not getting her to her place of there. Many times, the flame is never lit and you are trying to put it out.

What are you doing sleeping in another room with your door closed? Oh, the devil is a liar! Come out that corner. You can't hide. What if your wife needs you and she can't get your attention because you, no doubt, are wrapped up in pornography in another room? If that is not the case, then you are just too far away from her. Men, your responsibility is too great for you to be away. Paul says the husband is the head of the family as Christ is the head of the church (Ephesians 5:23). It also states that you are to love your wife the same way that Christ loved the church and gave himself for it. Husbands, you have got to give yourself to your wife. You've been holding back. Have you ever given her 100% of you? Tell the truth. Some of you got more secrets hiding from your wife than a single man. Would you faint if your wife got a hold to your billfold? I know you are saying she doesn't have any right to go into my billfold. Okay, I hope nothing unexpectant doesn't happen where she may have to for any reason. There are also cell phones which carry a lot of information. Suppose she needs to access it for some reason? Husbands, you have a great deal more responsibility in the marriage than the wife does. You are the leader and you both must take your place in God's order.

I admonish you to stop abandoning your wife. You don't support or look after her. She's left high and dry. You've turned your back on her, broken up with her, deserted her, ceased to love her, stopped having sex with her, and stopped having lovely things to say. To you pastors, it's time for you to get back to your bedroom.

MARRIAGE NUGGET #6

Warning Against Living Carelessly

God Is Not Pleased

Men of God, you who are unfaithful to your wife, are rocking and rolling high in your own boat and not the gospel of the Lord and God is not at all pleased with you. He sees and knows your heart, which is far from Him. You worship Him with your lip service. You preach truth, but you are far from living truth.

Now, Mother is not afraid to tell you the truth for everything will fail, but the truth of the Gospel. You need to take heed to your ways and stop mistreating your wife, which also affects your family. It seems as though all of a sudden your wife isn't smart enough, beautiful enough, but no what has happened is your lustful eye has become brighter and your scope for pornography is larger. Your appetite for the filthiness of the flesh has become greater. Your wife is the same woman you met and you have a lifelong duty to perform to her as long as she lives. That's the will of the Father. Stop mustering up love for the woman outside and not for the one inside who is your beloved wedded wife. Stop the sinning and practicing sin every day against your family. Your actions affect the children also. Children are hurt and confused wondering why daddy doesn't stay home anymore or why mommy and daddy don't get along or why daddy doesn't love mommy anymore or why mommy isn't happy anymore.

Don't go to hell with your eyes open.

Knowing the truth, teaching the truth, preaching the truth, yet not living the truth you are preaching about sends you to hell with your eyes open.

44 years ago, God called me to cry aloud and spare not; to lift my voice like a trumpet and show my people their transgression

and the house of Jacob their sins (Isaiah 58:1). It was on Friday night in 1971.

You know it is wrong to commit adultery, which is voluntary sexual intercourse between a married person and a person who is not his or her spouse also called infidelity, disloyalty, and extramarital sex. Yet, some live an adulterous lifestyle everyday in every season of the year. You have those who are your main squeeze and those who are seasonal tickets. There are just certain times you see them.

Some have outside mates/partners, life partners, lovers, companions, or significant others and having been with them for 9, 12,15, or 20 years or more. You are committed to them everyday such as you check in or run by everyday or you place a phone call or text. In other words, you spend more time with the outside mate than you do with your spouse. Remember, my calling is to cry aloud and spare not; to lift my voice like a trumpet and show God's people their transgression and sins.

God never meant for married people to be bed hoppers, exchanging partners—Why? It is a sin. 1 Corinthians 3:16-17 'know ye not that ye are the temple of God and that the Spirit of God dwelleth in you? If any man defile the temple of God, him shall God destroy: for the temple of God is Holy, which temple ye are.' This is a warning against sex sins, which destroy the body.

Galatians 5:24, and they that are Christ's have crucified the flesh with the affections and lust.

1 Corinthians 6:13, God has made appetite for food and food for appetite. Yet, he has not made the body for immoral acts, but for the Lord!

Genesis 2:24-25 therefore, shall a man leave his father and his mother, and shall cleave to his wife and they shall be one flesh.

Matthew 19:5, Ephesians 5:31, and Ephesians 5:25, you don't become naked until marriage: and they were both naked; the eyes of the Lord is upon you. Maybe your spouse doesn't see you, but God does and I have been sent to warn you to stop it.

MARRIAGE NUGGET #7

Husbands Return to Your Wives

God hates a divorce. Husbands, you are the chief of your household and priests of your home. Where are you? God says the woman's desire shall be to her husband (Genesis 3:16). No, but you aren't there and now Satan's sex demons are playing around her bed pretending it is you, but it is not you for you are out of place. You are, perhaps, in another bedroom or another woman's bed. God did not give the spirit of separation, but oneness between a husband and wife.

Prayer against the Spirit of separation

We command you to leave the heart of the husband and we command that his will be lost and the will of the Father be done. We pray for husbands to return to their wives and love her as Christ loves the church. He is not to defraud his wife, but to pay his matrimonial debt by meeting her needs and pleasing her. We pray the same prayer for the wife. In Jesus' name. Amen.

Married people, when crisis comes, bundle together instead of separate. Be wise, come together, and feel like you are against the world instead of each other. Know destiny brought you together and the Kingdom of God will be brought to earth by your victorious married life. Make the woman (your wife) in doubt disappear and restore trust and honesty in your marriage.

Listen, return now. Return to intimacy (into me you see) and be of one mind, one Spirit loving and devoted to each other. Don't retire on each other, but refire; get the fire burning again by falling in love over and over again. Keep your decision up to date that you are going to love your wife forever. As Jesus bought and purchased the church by giving his life so ought you man to see yourself as the purchaser of your wife to love her always. Fight for her instead of fighting her; becoming closer than close enabling her to laugh and not always cry unless she is crying tears of joy. During her baby birthing days, those days when she is pregnant, make her feel very special which she is. Let it be heaven on earth for her and not hell on earth.

God wants your marriage to be what His church is to him. He cherishes his church. Give your wife sensational moments, gratifying times, wonderful memories, and happy hours.

Return to calling her sweet names, romancing her, having date nights, and looking her up and down because she's all yours now. Remember, you bought her with your love; therefore, keep her at the center of your eye. Her heart is saying return, my love, return to me.

MARRIAGE NUGGET #8
No Roller Skating into Heaven

You are not going to heaven on your skates. Put on your holy shoes and walk in God's statutes—His word. Take off the skates; it is not your way that things are to be done, but it is God's way. There will be no slipping and sliding into the Kingdom. The clean and pure of heart will be there. Love and humility are there. Faith, kindness, gentleness, temperance, and long-suffering will be there and that lets us know to amend our ways and doings.

> Jeremiah 7:3-7
> Thus saith the LORD of hosts, the God of Israel, Amend your ways and your doings, and I will cause you to dwell in this place. Trust ye not in lying words, saying, The temple of the LORD, The temple of the LORD, The temple of the LORD, are these. For if ye throughly amend your ways and your

doings; if ye throughly execute judgment between a man and his neighbour; If ye oppress not the stranger, the fatherless, and the widow, and shed not innocent blood in this place, neither walk after other gods to your hurt: Then will I cause you to dwell in this place, in the land that I gave to your fathers, for ever and ever.

This is not to bring condemnation, but conviction to your soul to stop transgressing against your wife.

Romans 12:1 says,

I beseech you therefore, brethren, by the mercies of God, that ye present your bodies a living sacrifice, holy, acceptable unto God, which is your reasonable service.

Stop mistreating your wife and be not conformed to this world, but be ye transformed by the renewing of your mind, that ye may prove what is that good and acceptable and perfect will of God (Romans 12:2).

Men stop letting pornography be your ruin. You must remember sluts are in those videos, not classy and saved women. Stop coming home looking for animal and dog actions. Let your actions be gentle, loving, and intimate with your wife and go on to your perfect place called the heavenly bliss. You've been called to protect her—not to dog rape and fight her.

Learn how to minister to her. You are not ready for anyone else. You haven't mastered your wife yet, but you're out looking for another. It is lust. It takes all you got to keep who you're married to happy.

Some of you don't know how to please your wife. You never asked her what she likes. You just assumed and she just pretended in many cases. Make an effort to know what your wife likes and dislikes. She has a preference. Give her your attention and make her feel good and stop thinking about some other individual who is not yours. It is time to do it right according to God's way.

Where is your wife? How is she? Pastors, you have a God-given duty to your wife. Where is she? Or is there another and she no longer exists in your heart? Many times, they are still in your life, but not in the heart. I hear of so many negative sayings that God has not said such as I love her, but I'm not in love. Well, what or who are you loving? She is yours whether she does everything right or not; therefore, you are to love her as Christ has loved the church. He put a demand on you to love and cherish her as he has given himself for the church. Christ never made a distinction and loving the church, so love your wife as Christ loved the church.

Elders, ministers, deacons, bishops, apostles, you need to be examples for your family and congregation. Stop preaching what you preach and do what you want. Again, where is your wife? Has she been traded off for another? For God is not pleased with the divorce rate amongst those who proclaim to be blood washed and redeemed. Let's see what the scripture says about your attitude towards her.

For no man ever yet hated his own flesh; but nourisheth and cherisheth it, even as the Lord the church: For we are members of his body, of his flesh, and of his bones. For this cause shall a man leave his father and mother, and shall be joined unto his wife, and they two shall be one flesh.

– Ephesians 5:29-31

This is a great mystery, but I speak concerning Christ and the church. Nevertheless, let everyone of you in particular so love his wife even as himself and the wife see that she reverences her husband as her head. Where the husband is the head of the wife, even as Christ is the head of the church and he is the savior of the body. Therefore, as the church is subject unto Christ, so let the wives be to their husbands in everything that is lawful and right; not in things criminal in wrong. Be guided by the following scriptures as you return to your wives.

Colossians 3:19, husbands love your wives and be not bitter against them.

Matthew 19:5, cleave to your wives.

Ephesians 5:31-31, leave parents for wives and be joined as one flesh

Ephesians 5:29, cherish to warm in one's bosom; nourish and care and protect your wives; love your wives as you love your own bodies.

Ephesians 5:25, love your wives even as Christ loved the church and gave himself for it. Christ speaks to the husband to love his wife as he has loved the church.

Why is there so much abandonment? So many wives have been abandoned by their husbands including men of the household of faith which is in God's house. What is wrong men?

I honestly believe if you draw nigh unto God, He will draw nigh unto you. You must do your first work over and cleanse your hands and purify your heart and be not double-minded. You have been called with a holy calling (2 Timothy 1:9) not according to your works, but according to His purpose and grace to fulfill God's purpose in your life.

Romans 5:8, 'but God commendeth his love toward us in that while we were yet sinners, Christ died for us. 'This is how Christ loves. Where is your love for your wife? I know you won't die for her because you are failing to forgive her, remain faithful to her, and love her. Whatever is not right, you are her head; speak to that situation and cause it to come in alignment. If you walk right before the Lord, you can call these things that be not as though they were (Romans 4:17); walk upright to cause her to respect and honor you and cause God to stay with you. If she does not walk in obedience, you walk before God circumcised, so God can deal with her and surely, He will. Humble yourself also (1 Peter 5:5) and be clothed with humility for God resists the proud and give grace to the humble. Humble yourselves therefore under the mighty hand of God that he may exalt you in due time (1 Peter 5:6).

To cry aloud and spare not to lift my voice like a trumpet and show God's people their transgressions and sins is the charge God has given to me. You cannot roller skate into heaven on your own principles having disregarded the principles of God.

MARRIAGE NUGGET #9

Counsel Not Yourself

In my knowing that marriage was ordained of God to be a total commitment to one individual for a lifetime with unconditional love, that alone kept me in remembrance of my holy vows before a holy God. Knowing that it was not His will that my husband and I be in opposition with one another, but recognizing it was Satan, the adversary, who had come against our marriage opposing what God had ordained for us. I took marriage to be “where life begins and love never ends.”

I counseled not myself, but allowed the Word of the Lord to counsel me through my afflictions knowing that I would not always have to go through things. I would overcome and be a testimony if I kept the faith and endured the test. I knew I would be a witness of His great delivering power!

Therefore, I took on the fruit of the spirit: long-suffering; as a matter of fact, I had to bear all nine fruits for I realized I could not bear long-suffering and my trials without temperance, love, joy, peace, goodness, faithfulness, gentleness, and meekness. Those attributes of a Christian from the Apostle Paul to the Galatian Church stayed with me; therefore, I vowed to let them rule in my life (Galatians 5:22-23).

My being a chaste, born-again woman, I needed to exemplify the nine attributes of a Christian life which include the fruit of the Holy Spirit. I made a declaration and proclamation that they would have ownership over my flesh.

In my trying times, I would come under conviction with these scriptures:

- Blessed are the meek for they shall inherit the earth **(Matthew 5:5).**
- Blessed are the peacemakers for they shall be called the children of God **(Matthew 5:9).**
- Blessed are they who mourn for they shall be comforted **(Matthew 5:4).**
- Blessed are the merciful for they shall receive mercy **(Matthew 5:7).**
- Blessed are the pure in heart, for they shall see God **(Matthew 5:8).**
- Blessed are they who are persecuted for the sake of righteousness for their existing Kingdom of Heaven **(Matthew 5:10).**

Living out the beatitudes is very important for a Christian. I am convinced that the beatitudes of Jesus provide a way of life that promises salvation; they also provide peace in the midst of my trials and tribulations on this earth.

In Matthew 5:43-44, Jesus says, 'love your enemies; bless them that curse you; do good to them that hate you, and pray for them which despitefully use you, and persecute you.' These scriptures enabled me to surrender all. All to him I freely gave for he was my blessed savior and rewarder.

There was no way I could love my enemies and I could not continue to love my husband. I had to pray for them who despitefully used me, but one of them was my husband. I could not accept that, but I had to learn to pray for my husband when he mistreated me the way he did during those tough years. I held onto the word of the Lord along with letting my praise be my weapon.

Women, a strong woman in the Lord will work a challenge. My challenges helped to perfect me. What the devil meant for evil, God meant it for good. The enemy sought to use my challenges to take me out, but God said otherwise. I came to the conclusion that love and marriage are both sacrifices. When you are hurt, that's an opportunity to show love. Jesus suffered much, yet he loved.

I had received grace, then I wanted to be an extension of that grace; a giver and not just a receiver. Why not let my husband be that recipient in my life? My husband needed the grace that was put on me, and through the down pits of our marriage, I extended it to him with many acts of kindness. Our marriage was delivered by the grace of God. Patience had to have her perfect work in my life towards my husband.

One of the main ingredients in the marriage formula is obedience. Your blessings come from your obedience. Isaiah 1:19 let us know there are conditional blessings; v.19, 'If ye be willing and obedient, you shall eat the good of the land.' Through my obedience to God's word and to my husband, I am reaping the good of the land. My husband seeks to keep me happy and pleased.

As I write now, he is out making sure my car is in good shape by buying new tires for it. Early this morning, he washed my car for me. He also stopped by the restaurant to pick up our food for today and to the pharmacist. I love him for being so loving, but remember I loved him when he was not loving. Now, my paycheck is good and very good. Yes, he also pays the bills and finances me.

Now, he turns down the bed for me and in fact, he asked if I noticed that he made the bed and pulled the blanket back, and all I had to do was get in and cover up? He likes me to take notice of these acts.

Even on Valentine's Day, he wants me to know he still loves me. Even in his old age, he still reminds me that he loves me for the dreams we made come true. He is grateful for the years we have shared and that loving me has made all the difference.

MARRIAGE NUGGET #10

See God in Your Marriage

I chose to see God in my marriage. I wouldn't let the devil take God out. I remembered God was with us. God got bigger; my problems became smaller. Do not trust your soul to counsel you! For your counselor is in the blueprint of God's holy word. Marriage is till death do you part; not until you get tired of trying. You must not forget your wedding vows you made to each other. I must admit, I forgot my vows, but after getting saved, I remembered God's word. Therefore, I practiced God's word in my marriage. I hid the word of God in my heart and that was my survival kit.

Know this, that grace is the head of your house. Grace at supper everyday with prayers and faith. With prayers and faith, the power of united prayer, you can weather the storm. Again, I say unto you, that if two of you shall agree on earth as touching anything that they shall ask, it shall be done for them of My Father which is in heaven (Matthew 18:19).

You and your spouse came into agreement for marriage. The instruments came together; finally, they hit the same tune and note and you are married now. You made vows to each other and the charge is for you both to answer in judgment. Let your marriage be of a three-fold cord that is not easily broken. God, you, and your spouse are the majority for God hates a divorce. Yes, Moses gave a bill of divorcement, but it was not God's will.

There is no marriage without a cross. Jesus is the teacher, Holy Ghost, the enablement, and the Helper. Invite him into your marriage, which is ordained of God to be the cornerstone of life.

Matthew 19:3-8, the Pharisees also came unto him tempting him, and saying unto him, is it lawful for man to put away his wife for every cause? And he answered and said unto them have you not read that he which made them at the beginning made them male and female? And said for this cause shall a man leave his father and mother and cleave to his wife and they shall be one flesh? Where they are no more twain, but one flesh. What therefore God has joined together let no man put asunder.

They say unto him why did Moses stay in command to give a writing of divorcement in to put her away? He said unto them, Moses because of the hardness of your heart, suffered you to put away your wives with him, but from the beginning it was not so. Married vows are not to be broken; a man is to love his wife like he loves himself and as Christ loves the church.

I Chose to Stay

I knew God, not my vows. By my knowing God, my husband got to know Him through my lifestyle. His cry became the same as Ruth's in the Bible.

Entreat me not to leave or return from following you; where you go, I go; your God is my God.

–Ruth 1:16

He would voice to me that if I left him, he would be lost. I chose to stay. He felt confident with me. I pray my story will encourage other women not to throw in the towel, but let forgiveness have its perfect work in their lives; to wait on the Lord and experience His abundance of blessings for their marriage. I say to you to let healing come forth rather than divorce. The love of God and His healing touch will fix your marriage.

Facing Hardship

Though the storm clouds raged in my marriage, I took courage and I sailed on into my destiny. The thief (devil) comes to kill, steal, and destroy. The intent was to take from me. I could not afford to withdraw from my husband because the intent was to take from me. While I would have been withdrawing, the other woman would have been saying "Draw me nearer to you" or "I need thee every hour; Come right now my lover." The devil is a liar; don't let him have what's already yours—you can't have my husband was my decision. I also chose to forgive my husband.

Forgiveness is a decision; not an emotion. You got married and ended up in a storm. Wear the storm even when the wind is likened unto a whirlwind, typhoon, or hurricane blowing in all directions. Trust me, there is a way out! Let the Holy Spirit take you where you need to be. Jesus will be your life boat!

We are to emulate Christ in every area of our lives. On the cross, he said Father forgive them for they know not what they do. I learned how to forgive while in pain even when my flesh was being crushed, beaten, and crucified and my members were being put to death.

Know behind every promise, there is a principle. Don't be good at church, but bad at conflict. We must love like Jesus. The word of God took out my stony heart and gave me a heart of flesh. The only reason we have access to God's promises is because we've been forgiven. The reason you've been stuck is because you have unforgiveness in your heart.

Matthew 6:14-15, for if ye forgive men their trespasses, your heavenly father will also forgive you; but if ye forgive not men their trespasses, neither will your father forgive your trespasses. Don't just think on it. Act upon it. I took courage and sailed on into my destiny where I created a world of love and kindness for my marriage that God may draw my husband unto Him.

MY AWESOME END

My marriage was challenged by the devil and I won! My test became my testimony. I gave and it is being given unto me in good measure, pressed down, and shaken together, and running over. That is what my husband gives to my life. Indeed, my life is a product of Luke 6:38. My end results? What I measured out is being measured back. I survived 55 years of marriage with an adulterous husband through the word of God. The word of God has healing and life promises to it. My story is one of dying to the flesh and loving an unlovable husband. Maturity was birthed from it.

My book is part of my married life from 1962-2017. My beginning was full of loneliness, broken-heartedness, unhappiness, and infidelity. My end results? My husband serves me everyday as his royal wife. I encountered so much though. Now, I am reaping abundantly. I forgave the conflict as the Bible says and know that the blessing comes from obedience! God pays me well for my obedience! I am thankful! Through it all, I realize that the word of God is the final authority. The blood of Jesus gave me strength from day to day when I wanted to give up. It never loses its power!

After reading this book, I pray you will allow the word of God to counsel you. Trust Him and let patience have His perfect work in your life and marriage.

Love Always,
Mother Pearl J. Cole

AFTERWORD

Wow! Pastor Pearl Cole! You have made marriage to be honorable once again in the sight of the believers and not just the saints. What a blessing to finally see this lifelong lesson put into a book. I've heard, been in disbelief, but actually seen this book being manifested.

I can honestly say from the 10 to 12 years that I have personally known Pearl Cole, she has lived the scripture where the Lord is the Author and Finisher of her faith. She believed the word to the saving of her husband's soul. I know we talk about the scripture, 1 Corinthians 7:14, where the husband is sanctified through the believing of the saved wife, but she has proven that to be true. Pearl Cole has survived 55 years of marriage with an adulterous husband. She loved the 'hell' out of him—her husband (Smiling)! Now, he's a gentle and loving man of God! Nowadays, divorce is easy to most Christians, but she refused to be a statistic.

My desire is that this book, **How I Survived 55 Years of Marriage** *with an Adulterous Husband*, pulled you out of your seat of getting a divorce and gave you the courage to work it out. To God be the glory for what He has done for her. I'm so excited for you and the lives this book will, and has already, changed. Be blessed and prosperous through the days ahead.

Agape Forever,
Mother Andrea Carn

SPECIAL THANKS

I would like to extend special thanks, recognition, and gratitude to the Mothers and Missionaries who counseled and prayed for me.

- *Missionary Joan Barney*
- *Missionary Laverne Mobley*
- *Missionary/Mother Ella Watson*
- *Missionary/Mother Lonnie Mae Riley*
- *Mother Pauline Bright, Deceased*
- *Missionary June Sullivan*
- *Missionary Dorothy Fisher*
- *Missionary Gussie Wyche*

To request a catalog of available materials or to obtain information on having Pearl J. Cole as a guest at your church, conference, seminar, tent revival, or women's retreat in your community, please mail your request to the following address:

Pearl J. Cole Ministries, Inc.
P.O Box 26757
Jacksonville, FL 32226

Website: www.pearljcoleministries.com

E-mail: drpjcole@yahoo.com

ABOUT THE AUTHOR

Pastor Pearl J. Cole's life is a portrait. It may have been one of beauty or discord. 50 years ago in September 1966, the first Sunday of the month, she gave God her life and received him as her savior. She has not since looked back.

Pastor Cole's life as a mother, wife, minister, and pastor has firmly been established through time. As a mother, she has successfully raised seven children: Eugene Dwayne Cole, Recording Artist, Elder Andre Cole, Doctor of Praise, Sabrina Cole, Ph.D., Prophetess Darcelle Cole, Ph.D., Pastor Derrick Cole, Ph.D., Pastor Timothy Cole, DD, Troy Cole, Fire Fighter, and Minister Terrence Cole, Minstrel of Music. As a wife, she has dedicated 55 years of marriage to Eugene Cole.

As a minister, Pastor Pearl Cole received the title "A Worldwide Moving Woman." Known as a citywide evangelist with gifts of healing, deliverance in marriage, and the loosing of strongholds, the signs of God have followed this woman through time. During her years of evangelism, God has taken her to a higher dimension in the ministry working with her son, Pastor Timothy Cole and Prophet Brian Carn. She has appeared on the Word Network, Daystar Network, and Brian Carn Live twice with Prophet Brian Carn. Working with Prophet Carn's Prophetic Encounter and Visitation Conferences, she has become affectionately known as 'Mother Pearl' from Prophet Brian Carn's conferences.

To ensure that God's people are properly ministered to, Pastor Cole equipped herself the more in God and attended the Jacksonville Theological Seminary. She received a Bachelor of Arts in Christian Psychology, Master of Arts in Christian Education, and a Doctorate in Theology. This woman has met the requirements of mother, wife, minister, and pastor, and not just because of time, but also because of her dedication to her Rock, Jesus Christ.